HOLY

Finding God's PRESENCE
in Your Pain

Brian Morris

eLectio Publishing
Little Elm, TX
www.eLectioPublishing.com

Holy Crap: Finding God's Presence in Your Pain
By Brain Morris

Copyright 2016 by Brian Morris. All rights reserved.
Cover Design by eLectio Publishing. All rights reserved.

ISBN-13: 978-1-63213-142-3
Published by eLectio Publishing, LLC
Little Elm, Texas
http://www.eLectioPublishing.com

Printed in the United States of America

5 4 3 2 1 eLP 21 20 19 18 17 16

The eLectio Publishing editing team is comprised of: Christine LePorte, Lori Draft, Sheldon James, Court Dudek, Kaitlyn Campbell, and Jim Eccles.

Publisher's Note
The publisher does not have any control over and does not assume any responsibility for author or third-party websites or their content.

CONTENTS

ACKNOWLEDGEMENTS

This book is dedicated to the church body that encouraged me to keep writing, sustained me with prayers I often could not pray for myself, and lifted my hands when I was weak. I could never name all the people who have touched my life through the years and cannot find words to thank all of you for your never-ending support in so many ways.

To Lisa, my personal editor, for all the times you read and reread this book to make sure we could speak to all different people in all seasons of life. You are someone I trusted not only with my story but also with friendship and honest feedback. Yolanda and I love you, Mike, and all the kids deeply.

To my family, for your support and encouragement while I went through my challenges. I am the product of a family that would give anything to anyone, and my life is better because of the foundation of love and support I have always felt in my life.

And finally to Yolanda, my wife, for your support and prayers in so many ways and over so many nights when I was sick. I am a better man for having you in my life, not just as a wife but also as my best friend.

INTRODUCTION

Pain is relative. What is painful to you may or may not be painful to me, but one thing is constant with pain: when you are in it, you don't really care about what else is going on around you. Think about the times you have been really sick. Your number one priority in life is not the outcome of your favorite TV series or the ending to the book you are reading. It is for the pain to stop. And, usually, you will do anything to make that happen.

This book is for people who are in pain or are watching someone else in pain and for those who will go through pain. No one is really outside the reach of pain. At some point in your life, you will go through something, emotionally or physically, that will challenge you to a point of spiritual, emotional, or physical breakdown. In this book, I'm sharing the most terrible yet amazing, most horrific yet wonderful life-changing event that has ever happened to me.

This book is also for that person who may have lost touch with God through life's circumstances and the stresses that come from having terminally ill kids or from hearing a bad report from the doctor, when you feel as if you have done everything right in life and yet life is not fair. Maybe you just don't feel as if God is listening anymore, or you feel that He has *never* really listened when you were in need.

Well, I hate to heap on, but life is not fair in any way, shape, or form. Pain is only an opportunity to grow and become stronger so that you can change your little corner of the world for the better. That is why I am writing this book–to tell my story from the eyes of

1

a man who thought he was in command of his future and had done everything right in God's eyes–and thought he *had done* for a long time–and didn't think he deserved what happened to him. The title of this book is *Holy Crap: Finding God's Presence in Your Pain* because all of us have an opportunity to find God in the crap we go through. I call it holy crap because you make a decision that the difficulties you go through are going to make you stronger and that you are going to let God use them for good in your life and in the lives of others.

The Bible is such a powerful book; I have held onto it, and God has held onto *me* through it, so sometimes I am going to point *you* to it, too, in this book. In Hebrews 12:11, it talks about how there is a benefit to going through pain and suffering, but how we handle it is a choice that we need to make. Barnes Notes states–and I think it is a great way to put it–"…religion does not render him insensible to suffering[;] it does two things:

(1) it enables him to bear the pain without complaining; and

(2) it turns the affliction into a blessing on his soul. "Nevertheless afterward." In future life. The effect is seen in a pure life, and in a more entire devotedness to God. We are not to look for the proper fruits of affliction while we are suffering, but "afterward."[1]

I want to share my experiences in the hopes that they will help you if you are going through something right now or if you are watching someone you love go through hell. I may not know

---

[1] from Barnes' Notes, Electronic Database Copyright © 1997, 2003 by Biblesoft, Inc. All rights reserved.

exactly how you feel, but I do know what it means to have something unexpected and very painful (not to mention expensive) happen, causing you to feel like the world is falling apart. I know about the mind games the devil plays and the levels of hopelessness that would cause a little church boy (myself) from the capitol city of Montana to consider killing himself. I know about pain, but I also know about the hope brought by people I didn't even know who were praying for me when I couldn't pray for myself. And I know the priceless worth of having the **anchor** in my life known as Yolanda (my wife). I like to call her, "the woman who wouldn't let me quit."

People would tell me, "Brian, you need to find the peace that passes all understanding."[2] I would say, "That's what people who are NOT in pain tell people who ARE in pain." I do believe I found God's peace, but there is something else connected with that statement. The peace that passes all understanding comes with a price of great understanding. In other words, the peace that you want comes with understanding that you *need to trust God* to receive that peace. The peace you want comes with a price that must be paid, and that price is surrender. I learned, after four-plus years, that I was pretty crappy at that–surrender.

This book is not necessarily meant to be read quickly, as it is more for reading and reflecting on your own situation. Your progress through this book will probably also be based on your season of life. If you are in the middle of a life-altering situation, you will probably only be able to take a paragraph at a time, crying in between. When I wrote this book, I remember crying while at the

---

[2] Php 4:7

bookstore from the rush of emotions as I sat and typed. This book was very cathartic and important for me to get thoughts and feelings out of my head. As I was living out this experience, I had kept a notepad of things I could remember that I wanted to share in my book, and as I later typed from subject to subject, the pain became so vivid that I actually replayed the events in my mind as I was typing. I relived the never-ending office visits with multiple doctors who could not tell me the cause of my sickness, the nights of writhing in pain while lying in my bed and not being able to sleep, and the thoughts of committing suicide.

I am sure anyone who saw me, typing away in the corner of that bookstore, was wondering what in the heck was going on with this crying six-foot-six guy on a Saturday afternoon. Little did they know that I was preparing to share defining moments of my life with you, the reader, in the hopes that you would maybe hang on for one more day and that, maybe, by reading my book, it would help alter your thinking from being a victim of the crap of life to coming out a victor and learning lessons that could NEVER be learned in other seasons.

I have also included "Holy Crap Moments" for you to read and ponder and have added a few lines under each one, entitled "Take a Moment," where you can jot down thoughts that come to mind or list the things you want to work on. This could possibly start a healing process for you. I provided these sections in the book for you to stop and really consider where you are in life and the pain that you are going through, so don't be quick to read, write, and move on. Healing in life is a process, and I hope this book can be a tool to help you make progress in that journey or maybe start, or even restart, a relationship with God.

Chapter 1
Holy Crap! This Book is for Everyone!

In this book, I am addressing three basic groups of people. So I am talking to you if you are someone who doesn't know what in the heck I am talking about but were given this book because some kind of crap is happening in your life. I'm also talking to you if you were close to God at one time in life but something happened along the way to derail that relationship. And I'm talking to you if you have a relationship with Jesus, and life is generally going well, but you want to have a resource when life takes a turn for the worse in some way. (Plus, it is one CRAZY story!) I am not promising to have all the answers, but I do know that I have learned from the victories and failures of others and want to pass along to you the wisdom that I may have gained from the crap I went through for five painful and dark yet illuminating years. My goal is that the contents of this book can be applied in some useful way to help you know that there is hope before, during, and after the crap of life.

Something important I want to make sure you understand before you continue reading is my perspective on the cause of sickness and on dealing with pain. I know there are at least two sides to why pain happens in life. There is a camp that believes sickness is purely a direct attack from satan that is not a part of the natural order of our existence on this earth, while others believe that God allows things to happen to teach us life lessons that we would never learn without them. This book is not to try to help you decide whether pain and sickness is directly a demonic attack or if it's God allowing a necessary season of teaching. The only fact I want you to realize, no matter what theological standpoint you come from, is that, if you don't learn from the crap of life, it becomes purely a game of survival and not growth.

When I was kid, I would ride with my grandpa occasionally to a favorite lake to go ice fishing. I can remember one trip where I thought it would be fun to jump up and down on the cracking ice around the edge of the lake. I liked the sound the ice would make when I would jump up and down on it, not realizing how dangerous it was for me to be at the lake's shore on ice that was not completely frozen. I was right next to the shore and jumped way up in the air and came down on a piece of ice that gave way under my feet. I fell into the ice-cold water a good distance away from where my grandpa was sitting. The ice under my feet was like a slide under the water, and I couldn't keep my feet under me and started to slip under the ice. I tried climbing out of the lake but would just slip further into the icy water. I reasoned that all I could do was turn back out towards the middle of the lake and break the ice further away from shore until I could get out to thicker ice and climb out. I can remember thinking that I was going to die. Well, needless to say, I ended up pulling myself out and getting back to the safety of my grandpa. I learned a valuable lesson that day about icy conditions on a lake and did not try anything like that again.

I share this to help you understand something: when you are in the middle of crap, your primary thinking is to just survive. I understand the feeling of despair and the instinct of survival in an adverse situation. The fact is that, when you are in crap, you need to find a way out, and I believe that way is simply crying out and reaching out to others and God for help. Think of this fact: 100 percent of prayers not prayed are 100 percent of prayers not answered. You can lose nothing by praying and asking God to intervene in your life situation. When you get in the crap of life, whether it is God allowing it or a blatant attack from the devil, it is time to hang on, don't give up, and learn as many life lessons as you can. This book is me hanging on, not giving up, and learning life lessons then sharing what I feel God showed me to help others who are either going through crap now or will do so in the course of life.

Let's say you are reading this book because you thought it had a funny title, or you are going through crap in your life and someone gave you this book to read. Well, if you are not willing to be challenged, to cry a little, laugh a little, or just be encouraged not to quit but to go on for one more day, you probably should put this book back on the shelf or delete it from your Kindle or eReader. I want this book to pull back the curtain on a guy who thought he had life all figured out. See inside the mind and heart of someone who grew up being a good person (in his own mind) but who still went through pain like anyone else and who learned some *holy* crap along the way.

Maybe you don't have a relationship with God–you don't even know what that term means. I want to encourage you to have an open mind with this book as you read about my life experiences. Everyone has dealt with or will deal with pain in life, and this book is a quick snapshot of things I learned about my relationship with God and the importance of having people around you to lift you up when you are down and to help you navigate the sometimes incredible storms of life. Thank you for *not* putting this book back on the shelf or deleting it off of your eReader. You are in for one "Heaven" of a ride!

Maybe you are someone who had a relationship with God but got derailed by a life event. I really feel for you. From all the crap I went through, it would have been very easy to throw in the towel and give up on life–and give up on *everything*, really. I am glad that I can look back now and see things from a better perspective, but I can still remember the depths of despair as if they were yesterday. Before I got sick, I was the best at judging "your type of person." I would use the line, "we sure need to pray for so-and-so. They have 'strayed from the path'" and then I would continue to dish the dirt about their lives and the challenges they were going through. When I look in the Bible, I see the example that Jesus set for all of us, and it's a stark contrast to my actions, words, and attitudes back in those days.

I may say this more than once in this book because I feel strongly about it, but I want to formally apologize for Christians, including myself, who have acted as if they were above trusting God in the middle of their own crap while judging others who were trying to trust Him in theirs. I want to challenge you to do something. I want you to give a relationship with Jesus another chance. Look into finding a good Bible-believing, Jesus-centered body of believers who have some form of accountability in their gatherings.

As you will see in this book, without the church body of believers and a strong church family praying for me and lifting me up, I am not sure I would have survived to write this book right now. My best explanation of a healthy and functioning church body is a place where you can *give* your best (get involved, pray for the pastor, give of your finances, etc.) and *get* the best from people who will pour into your life to encourage you, challenge you, and help give your life a purpose that is greater than having a nicer car, a bigger house, and more stuff. It can also be a place where you can expect God to make up for church members who may get it wrong sometimes, including you!

I have heard so many horrendous stories from people who used to follow God or go to church, and it was that certain person in the church who came to them and said something stupid, and it altered the course of their life away from God. Have you ever said, "If that's what it means to be a Christian, then I don't want any part"? Sadly, you will not be the first or the last, and I want to help you to consider the power and importance of a group of believers in your life to help guide and direct you.

The best thing about a walk with God is that it's a personal relationship with Jesus, but it needs a healthy body of believers to help guide and direct personal growth in that relationship. It would be like having a child and leaving him to fend for himself and learn about life on his own. He would grow up and only learn to live life with a reactionary, "just stay alive" mentality that would shape and define his life. Followers of Christ who have walked away from the church and from God are in a difficult place, having to succeed on their own, including staying motivated to know and do what is right versus what feels good.

I think the devil works in two specific areas to get people separated from God: the *unknown* and the *alone*. Life has a way of keeping us distracted so that we think we don't need God. And the world puts such a huge emphasis on a person's own ability to control and adjust their identity and direction for life without the help of others and God. When pain hits that is greater than the internal focus and controlled breathing a person has been taught, it is hard to keep it all together. When we do not know or understand who we are in Christ and the authority we have as followers of His, the devil uses that ignorance to push us into a corner. The result is that we think the devil has the upper hand and that we have no control over what happens. That is a lie, and it is the devil operating in the *unknown.*

When you think there is no need for accountability in your life and you try to live life without the influence of people loving you, encouraging you, and praying for your greatness, you are in the *alone,* and that is exactly where the devil wants you. This life was never meant to be lived alone, and the fact that Jesus told his followers in the Bible[3] to "not stop meeting together" was possibly insight into the level of crap humans would have to endure on earth. He knew that we would all need a personal relationship not only with Jesus but also with others to help us up when we are down or to remind us about how much Jesus loves us and that we have His authority in our lives as a resource.

I used to be the type of person who said, "If you are not ready to see the summit of where you want to be and strive to get there, then don't even start." But now I can say that I just want to be the type of person who helps people take just one more step in life and not give up on a relationship with Jesus.

I started running a few months ago and had a small revelation about people who don't think they can run extended distances. Someone asked me about being able to run and he said, "I could never run that far and not pass out." I told him, "You will never be able to run as far as you want until you run as far as you can." It was so weird because it just came out of my mouth and has ended up being an encouragement to myself in all areas of my life, including my relationship with Jesus. Just start with what you can do, and don't stop trying. Eventually you will see yourself running

---

[3] Heb 10:25 (NIV)

with Jesus further than you could have imagined and in better mental and spiritual shape than you could have ever dreamed.

Even as I type this chapter, I had a pretty terrible scare two weeks ago because I thought my eye was flaring back up and that the whole process of going blind and of sickness as a lifestyle was restarting. For a while, I was terrified. The devil wanted to push me into a corner again and make me think all over again that he had the upper hand and I was helpless and had no control over what was happening. But I am **not** helpless—and neither are you if you have committed your life to following Jesus. This is exactly how the devil tries to move in the *unknown* and use our emotions to take control. Even though I felt like it was something I needed to experience to help show me what it feels like to think you are completely on the other side of a crap event in life and then think that it is starting all over again, I knew I had to resist those lying symptoms that were trying to come back.

I am not sharing this to make it worse for you and your situation. I only want to illustrate the fact that life is unpredictable, but I serve and follow a God who, as it is stated in the Bible in Psalms 46:1 KJV, is predictably a "refuge and strength, a very present help in trouble." This same sure-footed strength and authority can be yours, too, if you just ask God for His help in your life, no matter where you are or what you are dealing with.

I think people who trust in or have a relationship with God and then walk away do so because of an unmet expectation. You may have been told that if you would do it all right and surrender everything to God, that nothing bad would or could happen to you. You were trying to have faith, but then a painful, unrelenting chain of events just beat you to the point that you eventually gave up. Or you went through something painful in life, tried to have faith, felt like you survived it, and started to regain some connection to God, and it came back again with the same flood of emotions and the power to take your breath away. And you said, in your head, "I am done." I will never tell anyone that I know what you are going through, but I do know how to pray for you if you're in that situation. If this book can help you just take one simple step back towards God, it was worth the years of going into debt, doubting God, hating where God had my life, and being in misery in general for all the years I was sick. You were worth it.

Then again, maybe you currently have a relationship with Jesus but you want to fortify your relationship with Him and have a resource for when life takes a turn for the worse. If you are in this group and you're reading my life story, then you may have had a problem with the title of my book. I have been discouraged more than once from calling it "Holy Crap" by well-meaning people in the church who thought the title was a bit too irreverent. I know this is a blanket statement, but I wanted to explain the title to people who have a relationship with God and may not understand why I named my book this way. Holy Crap, to me, is more than a title of a book. It is more like a renaissance or awakening in my life from who I was before I got sick to who I am now because of the many things I learned, going through sickness and finding the *holy* in my crap.

I know that not everyone who sees the title of this book automatically judges it, but sometimes people who are believers in Jesus are good at a couple of things: comparing and judging. Neither of these is considered positive, unless it has to do with comparing ourselves *to Christ* or judging *ourselves* before we notice or judge the actions of others. If you have a relationship with Jesus and nothing really negative is going on in your life, then that is great. Please see this book as a reminder that difficult things will happen in life and that you don't have to be reactive or overwhelmed by the circumstances of life. The times when we feel like everything is going well need to be times of getting closer to God to prepare for the attacks of the devil and fortifying the relationship we have with Jesus. This is not a defeatist mentality; it's just coming from someone who thought if he did all the right things, said all the right things, and was striving for *total* righteousness in life, that nothing bad would happen to him—which is false.

The crap I went through in life did not negate or refute the truth in the Bible, nor did it negate all the things I learned as a kid growing up and then as a pastor for ten years. But it did challenge how vitally connected I was to those truths. When we study the Bible and have a consistent prayer life (conversations with God), we are not working on making biblical truths more truthful. Those times should be for connecting us more deeply and personally to those biblical truths. I can say I learned, through crap in my life, that the truths in my mind and heart were disconnected from my ability to practically apply those truths in my life. Maybe I believed them in my head, but they hadn't been made *mine* in my heart.

Being on both sides of sickness, I can say it is paramount that believers are reinforcing the application of biblical truths and not just knowing and assenting to them with your mind. You start with believing them in your heart and then acting on them as though they really are true. God has provided us with all the tools to get through anything in life and has promised that we would not be given anything we could not stand up under. The only thing standing in the way of God's will being done in our lives and our walking in success, no matter what the devil throws at us, is our free will. I pray that you read this book and that it helps raise the importance of a connection between what you know, what you believe, and how you apply those truths to your life.

This book is for a person who is a seasoned Christian in the middle of something completely devastating, but it's also for someone who is still on a spiritual journey to find meaning in life and who continues to find dead ends in areas that are supposed to bring happiness and fulfillment in life. I have found that having a relationship with Jesus doesn't mean I automatically deal with pain well, but I do have the ability to deal with it in a constructive way. Come on a journey with me and maybe learn a little something about yourself along the way. It will help you start to trust God again and change the inevitable crap in your life to *holy* crap.

I have also set up a website at HolyCrapBook.com for you to consider for help. It can be a place to occasionally go see posts to encourage you or to read stories of people dealing with some of the same struggles you do. It will be a place where we can continue the conversation, even after you have read my story, to help you know you are not alone! We will also provide some thoughtful questions there, corresponding to each chapter, so you can continue a conversation on your own with others who may need a lifeline in *their* crap. So are you curious about this life issue I went through? Let's get started with the week that changed my life.

Chapter 2
How One Week Can Change a Life

I can remember the week when everything started as if it were yesterday. It's a funny thing about pain; you remember it for the rest of your life. There are reasons why we need to learn from pain and should actually work NOT to forget the lessons we learn from pain. I'll get into that later in this chapter. Even as I talk about pain, I am sure you have a specific instance in your life that you probably haven't addressed in a while. Perhaps you are currently in the throes of a very painful and earth-shattering situation that you feel others don't understand.

Holy Crap Moment:

Even though it is hard to realize when you are in the midst of pain, please remember that people who may not understand what you're going through should not be excluded from loving you and caring for you. Work on letting others love you. Maybe take a first step and simply say these words: "I choose today to let others love me."

Take a Moment

_____

_____

_____

_____

I was a spiritual leader of teens, or youth pastor, in the prime of my life, dealing with all of the normal things a pastor deals with on a weekly basis–solving emotional teen issues, encouraging kids to love one another and not be so clique-y, and encouraging them to listen to their parents because parents have a wealth of knowledge (at the very least) from the years they have spent on this earth. There was one week, though, that especially sticks out in my mind and that really changed the course of my life forever. I have had many people tease about pastors just sitting around their office, reading books all day and drinking lattes. The funny thing is that those people are not with me when I get phone calls in the middle of the night or on days off from people who need to connect with a pastor right away or who need a word of encouragement that says everything is going to be all right.

On Monday, I had a family call me about a problem they had with their teen. The teen had run away and was getting into drugs and alcohol. I dealt with the situation and let the family know I would be praying for them and would follow up that week to see how everything was going. On Tuesday, I had another parent call me and tell me that her pregnant teen, who had recently moved back in with them, was having some issues following the family rules and also needed me to connect with her. I thought, "Man, this is going to be an interesting week." I went over to their house and talked to the girl and her mom and really had a "God conversation" with them.

A God conversation is a talk that goes beyond my wisdom, in which all I do is put myself in the right place and God helps the people I'm talking to because I simply showed up and asked Him to work in the situation. Unfortunately, these times don't happen as often as they should when you are a youth pastor and think you have all the answers and that, because you have been a good kid your whole life, you have the answers for "wayward people" and the poor decisions they make. Needless to say, I know that the pain I have been through has brought a different perspective to me now, regarding my role in people's lives. As I get older, I also see that the only real value I have for people is because of the experiences I have gone through and that I must point them to Jesus in theirs. In myself, I don't have enough of whatever they think I can give them to get them through.

On Wednesday of that week, my mom called me and asked if I would pray for my grandpa because he was not doing well and the doctors thought he was going to die before the end of the week. This was not a complete shock to me but was still a little jarring considering the events of the week and the fact that I was also in the middle of getting ready for a youth retreat that weekend. Then Thursday came. It was almost as if I was waiting by the phone for the next thing to hit that week. When we are sick or going through crap in our lives, it is easy to have the attitude that we are just waiting for the next thing to happen. We get pessimistic about our circumstances–almost expecting the next unraveling moment to occur and take us on the next speeding plunge on the roller coaster of crap.

I think our human nature is automatically bent towards expecting the worst, but it's made even worse when we don't feel good, emotionally or physically. Pain is like THE monkey wrench that gets thrown into the workings of our lives. I also think it can be even more jarring if you feel as if you have done everything right in life and that you don't deserve whatever it is you end up dealing with, mentally or physically.

Holy Crap Moment:

---

*No matter what you are going through in life, stop expecting more **bad** to happen and start expecting the **good**. Commit right now to not having an attitude of expecting the worst or the other shoe to drop in life, even though you may be going through a huge test. I know this is easy for me to say, but it is the first step to getting through the crap in your life with something good to show for it. Nothing positive has ever come out of expecting bad, but when you are looking for the positive and for things to get better, you improve your outlook on life and change your focus from the crap you are going through to being grateful for even the smallest things. Right now, if you are going through some kind of crap, take a minute and write down three positive things in your life.*

Take a Moment

_____

_____

_____

_____

You will see references to the Bible in this book, and there is a very good reason to use this very valuable book when you are in the crap. Even though I was obstinate many times when people would give me a Bible verse (because I was so mad at God), it didn't change the truth contained in the Bible. This book is as much about learning from my mistakes as it is hearing my story of pain and being able to relate. The greatest mistake I made when I was sick and going through my situation was not leaning on the Bible as a guidebook for life as much as I should have, because I've known the power of it at other times in my life and have even seen how it has helped countless adults and students that I have been connected to through the years. Honestly, after about the twentieth bad report from the doctor that my medication was not working, I was regretting the fact that I would possibly be blind eventually, with at least one eye removed, and *not able to read the Bible anymore.*

I remember a member from our church and her mom stopping by my house and dropping off food for Yolanda and me. I got into a conversation with them and started to cry because I admitted that one of the things I would miss the most if I lost my sight was not being able to read the Bible. Please learn from my mistake of not incorporating the Bible and its rich truths into your life. Do not simply form negative opinions of what others may say about the Bible until you have read what it says for yourself. You can start about two-thirds of the way through, in the book of John. There is so much gold and life-giving truth in the Bible that can help your focus in the middle of the darkest, crappiest, most hurtful times of life.

In Romans 12:2, it talks about how the mind naturally needs to be renewed to God's truth. Look at this comment about the power and importance of the mind. It's really where the devil focuses his attacks of fear and hopelessness that are so unrelenting and brutal sometimes. The mind is the acting, ruling part of us; so that the renewing of the mind is the renewing of the whole man, for out of it are the issues of life.[4] Matthew Henry further explains:

> The progress of sanctification, dying to sin more and more and living to righteousness more and more, is the carrying on of this renewing work, 'till it be perfected in glory. This is called the transforming of us; it is like putting on a new shape and figure[5]

On Thursday morning, I received a phone call from my scheduled guest speaker for the youth retreat that weekend who said he couldn't come. That meant that I was going to have to come up with two evening messages and two small-group sessions in about thirty-six hours. It was not his fault that he had to cancel, as he needed to help someone in the group of kids that he ministers to and connects with in downtown Denver. I was not angry at all about the information, but as that became the next zinger phone call that week, my stress level catapulted and my mind began grasping for solid ground on which to get these messages and small groups lessons done. So I got to work on the messages and counted that as one of the craziest weeks of phone calls in my entire career as a youth pastor.

The next evening, Friday, I began leading the youth retreat. My mom called me that night and told me my grandpa had died and that I needed to come up to Montana for the funeral that was going to be on Monday, right after my retreat weekend. I finished my

---

[4] Prov 4:23

[5] *Matthew Henry's Commentary on the Whole Bible: New Modern Edition,* 1991

Saturday night service with my students and drove back to Denver that night, to leave for Montana the next morning. It was quite a whirlwind week that culminated with a funeral for my grandpa, which I helped officiate.

When I got back from Montana later that following week, I noticed something interesting with my left eye. I was looking in the mirror one day and noticed that a large vein had popped out in the lower left white part of my eye. It looked weird, but I didn't really think anything about it because it didn't really hurt. I knew there was something wrong with my eye, but I didn't really want to deal with it because it didn't hurt and I was busy with life. Sound familiar? How many things in our lives do we know are just not quite right, and we continue to do nothing about them because they don't really hurt? These can be physical or emotional in nature, and they need attention, but, because they don't hurt at the time, we don't deal with them.

Holy Crap Moment:

If you have a hurt in your life, deal with it. Don't ignore the fact that it needs attention. Maybe you have a good Bible-believing church that you should go back to and forgive people for the hurt they caused you. Maybe you have a stressed relationship with God and need to start talking to Him again. He is always ready to listen. Start the conversation. Maybe you need to get some professional counseling for a pain in your life that happened when you were younger, and, when you think about it, you are at a loss for words. I believe that my eye situation was a type of problem-ignoring, and I'm hoping that, by reading this book, it will help jar you out of a lack of care for life or a lack of dealing with personal issues that need attention.

Take a Moment

_____

_____

_____

_____

I continued on with my life after that week and didn't really think anything about my eye until it started getting more red and irritated. I went to an optometrist in town, and he told me that I had scleritis, which is an inflammation of the white part of my eye. That was the beginning of innumerable and costly doctor visits, countless bottles of medication, a restrictive and precisely-regimented daily schedule of pill-taking, and unending sleepless nights with a wandering mind that only thought the worst about what was going to happen. At that early stage, my mind could never have dreamed of the intense pain and deep levels of depression I was to go through in the next four years. It was a journey that would test everything inside me and help show this good little church boy that he had a very limited knowledge of who God was in the darkest hours of his life.

Now back to my statement I made at the beginning of this chapter: we remember pain. To me, it is a guaranteed fact that we remember pain and everything that goes along with it. We remember faces, environments, smells, and even the times of day when pain hits. For months, when I was really sick and staying home every day, and Yolanda was going to work during the day, I remember being hit with horrendous times of despair from 2:30pm until about 5:00pm every day. I would dread those two-and-a-half hours of my day more than the rest. It may have been bad because that was about the time of the afternoon when my eye would start to become red, headaches would kick in, and the medication I was taking would stop working. This was the time my mind would wander, and I would play out every terrible scenario that came to my imagination, from having my eye removed to going completely blind to dying.

Even as I type this, I have vivid and specific memories of this time in my life. My despair was so deep that I remember taking showers with my eyes closed so I could practice washing myself when I eventually went blind. I would also walk around my house with my eyes closed, memorizing where everything was so when I was blind, I could get around without Yolanda's help. I remember the fear of not being able to drive anymore. Every day during the week, I would drive my truck to the local grocery store and buy one item. It was nothing ever too expensive or needed–just an excuse to make a trip out of the house in my truck. This would be part testing to see if I could still drive and part finding something to do when I was stuck at home, obsessing about my future and the problems of my life.

I do believe that God takes away the sting of pain in our lives as it says in Isaiah 41:10, "So do not fear, for I am with you; do not be dismayed, for I am your God. I will strengthen you and help you; I will uphold you with my righteous right hand."[6]

We can also be healed from crap that happens, but we are still human and do not forget about things that happen to us because

---

[6] NIV Translation

God is not in the business of deleting painful situations from our minds. We can live a fulfilled and complete life of freedom with the memory of painful days but from the perspective of overcoming them and not being held in bondage mentally by them. In the introduction to the book, I referenced Hebrews 12:11 and the fact that we need to learn from the pain. If we don't learn from the pain we go through, then we just have pain and not a time of growth.

There are some checkpoints you can reference to see if you have learned from your pain. First of all, have you forgiven those specific people who have hurt you? If you cannot forgive someone for hurting you, no matter what it was, you give that person power over your life and the ability (without their knowledge) to continue to cause you pain. That's power they should never have and you should never give them. I had to work on forgiving God for what I thought He did to me. I had to consider what He was teaching me instead of just being angry from the circumstances in my life. I really believe this anger came from my own justification and trusting in my own righteousness because of all the "good things" I had ever done in my life, so I didn't think I deserved this kind of treatment. I was deceiving myself all those years and now was faced with a question of whether I believed in this God whom I had served since I was little.

Second, when you think about the crap you went through or are going through, can you think of how it made your life better, not worse? Are you looking at the circumstances you went through or how you matured through your situation? The awesome thing about pain (funny thought, huh?) is that you have an amazing opportunity to become a new person by going through it. In the Bible, Paul could see the power that comes from pain and the ability to become a better person in 2 Corinthians 12:9-10: "But He said to me, My grace is sufficient for you, for My power is made perfect in weakness. Therefore I will boast all the more gladly about my weaknesses, so that Christ's power may rest on me. That is why, for Christ's sake, I delight in weaknesses, in insults, in hardships, in persecutions, in difficulties. For when I am weak, then I am strong." (NIV)

I am not saying that pain is something good and should be encouraged, but I am saying that, because it is inevitable in life, we have an opportunity to make the quality of our lives better from it. Pain can be seen as an obstacle to overcome or an opportunity to grow stronger as a person. If you only consider pain an obstacle, then you will not see or learn the lessons that can build an insight into endurance that you would never learn in times of peace in life.

Lastly, are you willing to speak the truth of the Bible over your life and trust God for His strength when pain happens again in order to learn even greater things about yourself? Even though I am on the other side of the pain with my eye situation, this is one I am still working on. Really, this is not telling God, "I like pain so please give me as much as you think I need–and, oh, by the way, thanks a heap for it." Pain and death in life are not an *if* but a *when*. We live in a body that started dying the first day we were born. One day we will die, and our physical bodies will corrode and turn to dust. Fighting those painful situations with truth and the Bible is realizing that life is sometimes about going through pain. The only way I know how to do this is to have a loving and completely trusting relationship with Jesus. When I know God has my best interests in mind and wants me to be better than I could ever be without Him, then I will go through anything, not blame Him, and

I will get something really great out of it because I am keeping my eyes on Him and on the promises in the Bible.

Consider this: Your true make-up is who you are at your greatest point of weakness. If it doesn't do anything else, pain will show what you really believe and how much you need to learn about yourself. If you learn from your pain, it can be a marker of where you are going with God and with your life in a positive way. If you don't learn from your pain, it will be a constant reminder of where you have been and the negative impact that pain was on your life. It can cause you to give up, to be a negative person whom no one will want to be around, and can push away everyone who loves you because of your actions and attitude.

Think of it this way: painful situations will either be looked **at** or looked **from.** When you look AT a painful time or a scar in life, you fix your eyes on it and do things in your mind to evaluate and try to explain why you went through that, essentially losing the joy of your "now" in life. You stay stuck in your past and lose out on the joy of your present. When you look FROM something, you can still see the scar, but you notice how far you have come from that time in your life. Which kind of person do you want to be? Do you want to be someone who looks at life with hope and a purpose or someone who sees life as a series of unwanted and hurtful events that only lead to more pain? If you are the latter, there is hope for you. If I haven't scared you off by now, keep reading and see if God

> When you look FROM something, you can still see the scar, but you notice how far you have come from that time in your life.

doesn't do something really great in you. It's time to stop complaining about your circumstances and start finding God's presence in your pain. Start finding the "holy" in the inevitable crap of life.

I know that the pain I share about in this book may not be as bad as other people's pain situations, but it is my story of what I believe God taught me through my experience and the things that I believe I am still working on, even after coming through the greatest test of my young life. I want to be transparent about my failures and my victories, and if I can help just one person, it will have been worth taking the time to document my journey so people can read it and learn from it.

Chapter 3
The Definition of C.R.A.P.

I know this is not the most religious sounding title for a book, but it was what I felt I was going through for four-and-a-half years. I want to take this chapter to share with you what my definition of C.R.A.P. is. Besides the obvious definition that most people associate with this word, I really cannot think of a word I used more in my conversations with God while going through the level of pain I was in with my eye.

As I look back now on the life of pain I experienced, I can see the *holy* in the *crap* I was going through. I understand a little more about God using what happened to me for my greater good, but when I was dealing with everything first-hand, I did not see the gold and refinement that would come afterward in my life. I was probably more interested in knowing that what I was going through was all for a greater purpose than in needing to know the cause behind why such a lifestyle change was happening for Yolanda and myself. I definitely didn't want to feel as if my eye was exploding out of my head, but in some way, if I knew it was for a greater purpose, it would be tolerable. The only key problem with this thinking is that we don't always know the reason or the meaning to painful situations of life.

Holy Crap Moment:

I have a "why" within a "why" for you. Take a Moment right now and think about WHY you think you need to know WHY something bad is happening to you. Is it about control in your life

29

which you need to give to God or is it maybe a trust issue? God wants to help give you what you need for this journey called life, but if you cannot give Him total control of who you are and what you do, then you will stay frustrated with a hybrid version of following Christ that doesn't work. Either God is in control, or He is not.

Take a Moment

_____

_____

_____

_____

As humans, we always want to be in control and not have situations where we don't understand the reasons why. It's almost as if we can find a source or foundation for the reason something is happening, then it is just a little more palatable to us. I might be saying something different right now if the doctors had actually had to remove my eye, but this is what I can say is going through my head as I reflect on the years of teaching (as I so affectionately like to call everything that happened to me).

So lets get into the C.R.A.P., shall we?

"C" stands for *Consistent.* God knows that I am the type of person who only learns when there are no more ways of learning something. My wife has commented through the years about how she would tell me something that was for my own good, but I would not really listen to her at the time. Then, after a process of teaching two or three other ways or someone coming to me and saying the exact same thing, I would have a conversation with

Yolanda and would tell her of this new revelation that I had about said topic. She would just look at me and say, "Uh–didn't I just tell you that last week?" We would laugh and move on. Because I am this way with learning in life, I had to come to the end of myself by facing possible removal and excruciating pain in my eye for four-and-a-half years in order for me to learn some important principles.

Looking back now, I firmly believe that, if I had given in and had stopped complaining and trying to figure it all out, I probably would not have had to go on for so long with this disease. Consistent pain is something in your life that, at the time, does not seem as if it will ever end. I remember thinking that I would never really be able to travel and that I would have medical bills for the rest of my life. When I was at the stage of giving myself injections of Methotrexate in the leg, I thought that was as close to the end as I could get, when in reality, that was only the beginning of the drugs I would take and the doctors I would see over the next few years.

We allow the devil victory in our lives when we let him keep us farsighted on the PAIN in life (making us think painful crap will never end) and nearsighted on the PLAN that God has for our lives (making us think God doesn't have a plan to teach us something greater than the things we know at present). Don't let your eyes be kept on the pain of now or let that seep into and affect the idea of having an actual future that doesn't involve pain and taking drugs and seeing doctors on more than a periodic check-up basis.

Consistent pain will bring you to the end of yourself. It will test the very core of who you are and will do all the pruning that is needed for the life that God desires for you to have. God used the events of my life to teach me some very valuable lessons about myself and the things I thought I believed for a very long time. Now that I am on the other side of consistent pain, I must now live out what I learned through my eye situation—"And I know that when I have painful times in my future, God loves me enough to be right there for me, to show me the way of escape through Him"[7] – and through it all, I will keep learning valuable lessons. Just because painful opportunities to learn present themselves in life doesn't mean education is always a byproduct. My relationship with Jesus gives me the benefit of knowing I have a resource not only to help get through pain in life but also to learn from those opportunities and be better on the other side. I want to be a quick study concerning pain and the life lessons I learned, which I will share at the end of this book.

"R" stands for *Real*. Real pain in life is just what it says: real to the person going through a difficult situation. I used to think the greatest level of *real* pain was going to the dentist. I don't know why I have such a phobia about this, but it is still something I really don't like. In fact, I don't know many people who like those trips either. Now that I have faced the prospect of losing my eye and possibly having whatever was wrong in my body spreading to other vital organs and eating them away, or losing my house, being bankrupt, and fearing I would never preach again, I can say those things are my new standard of *real* pain. I am not saying that the pain I experienced was any worse than anyone else in the world, but it is definitely a way for me to empathize with others who go through pain in their lives. And more importantly, my experience is helping

---

[7] 2 Cor 10:13 (NIV)

me be better at listening to the people God has put in my care and trust as a pastor.

We are in a world that is looking for people to be real. Real with words, real with relationships, and real with general direction for life. What better way could God have prepared me to reach those people than to give me far greater compassion by going through a real pain that doesn't happen to very many people? As a result, not only do I know how to talk to others going through their own situations, but I also have a level of empathy to believe for a supernatural touch of God and a sense of hope that they could never experience on their own.

Holy Crap Moment:

Think about how you want people to be real with you when you are dealing with pain, and do the same for people you come in contact with who need a person to be real in their lives.

Take a Moment

_____

_____

_____

_____

"A" stands for Appropriate. At the time, I absolutely didn't think it was appropriate: the level of pain I was experiencing in the sleepless nights, the countless doctor visits–and bills to accompany those chats -- the thoughts of suicide, the hopelessness of being a failure to Yolanda as provider of the family, and overarching thoughts of a generally sucky life. I was so mad at God and felt so let down and abandoned by Him because I thought He was allowing these things to happen to me. I believed I was owed a better life, and because I thought God should get me out of my circumstances immediately–but apparently didn't want to (or so I thought) -- I began to think that God's "better" plan for me was to suffer this way and give in to His harsh ways.

But God is a loving Father, and He would never do that to people. He aches when we are suffering. He made a way out for me and you; I just didn't quite recognize it yet. God always has everything under control, even when we think our lives are spinning out of control. We need to realize that when crap happens in life, that it is appropriate for us to keep our eyes on Jesus and His power. The true test of our connection to God is going to be how quickly we begin to speak faith and to trust in His ability to bring out the best in every situation. The devil hates you and will always try to get you to settle for less than what God has for you, every time.

Holy Crap Moment:

What is the first thing you turn to for comfort when in pain? Is it God? Is it alcohol or drugs? Is it a friend or family? Is it self? The things we turn to while in pain will fully determine who or what we trust to help get us through pain. Learn to turn to God, and start by asking Him for help. He is just a prayer away. Maybe say this quick prayer; "God, I don't know where to start, but I want to turn to You FIRST when things go wrong in my life. Please help me, and please put people in my life to help direct me to You. Thank You for having my situation under control, and I release it to You in my mind and my actions. Amen."

Take a Moment

_____

_____

_____

_____

I am not saying that we should be doing double back-handsprings when crap happens in life, but I will say that we can have an attitude of trust in God when those things do hit. To me, the greatest testimony is not the person who has been through something and can talk about what they learned after the fact, although it is always good to positively reflect on how far you've come. The greatest testimony is the person who is still going through pain and still has faith and trust in God to either heal them and their situation or to carry them through the pain, and people watch how they deal with it in a godly way. I believe humans need not know the level of pain they will have to endure but instead work daily on their trust level with God. In that way, when the pain comes, they feel that what they are going through is appropriate, no matter what it is.

The last letter is the most important of all of these points: **"P,"** **which stands for Personal.** Personal pain is not how other people view what you are going through; it represents the deepest parts of your heart and mind, where no one goes except for you. This was the area of my mind and heart that I hung out in the most when I was sick and in despair. I feel this is what prompted my thoughts of suicide and the desire to end my life. It was why I wanted to come to church ten minutes late and leave five minutes early, so I didn't have to talk to anyone. The personal side of pain is the point at which other people cannot go and say, "I know how you feel." It's the side of pain that makes us feel as if no one has it as bad as we do or probably ever will. This is stuff we can keep hidden from other people when all the other areas of our life seem normal.

My affliction was my eye, so everyone who looked at me knew what I was dealing with. Maybe you have a wound in your heart or life that no one can see on the outside. Personal pain can be emotional, not just physical. Worst case scenario for me, they remove my eye, and I have a glass eye and eventually die from major organs being eaten from an overactive immune system. You cannot remove emotional or mental scars from the past or maybe even the present.

I really want this book to be a type of journey-starter for you who are dealing with emotional pain and scars that feel so personal that no one will understand. I know I had emotional issues with being able to trust God that He had everything under control, and I had felt fairly secure in my walk with God before I got sick. I know I am still a work in progress, as we all are, but I ask that you really consider things you are dealing with in your mind and heart and ask God to reveal things to you as you read on.

So if I had called my book Holy "Consistent, Real, Appropriate, and Personal" Pain, I may have had more people accept the title. However, I want to give people a better idea about how I really felt, as a church kid all my life, dealing with a God that I had to surrender to and learn life lessons from that were invaluable for a truly successful future on this earth and in eternity. After dealing with consistent, real, appropriate, and personal pain, I now know God has developed me in those areas for the better. God wants me to be <u>consistent</u> with people I meet and, in love, listen to their hurts and pain. He wants me to be <u>real</u> with all generations I talk to without having to say, "I know what you are going through." He's helping me to have an <u>appropriate</u> level of trust in Him so I can let Him teach me deep things in painful situations, and He is expanding my <u>personal</u> relationship with Jesus, not just as a pastor under the title of Pastor but as a true man of God.

Crap in life is what we make it. You have an opportunity to allow your circumstances to direct your life or for your life to be a result of the things you learn from the pain that comes. Life is just a series of decisions, and your pain is just another opportunity to allow yourself to grow in this life in a positive way.

Chapter 4
Overcoming a Pain-Controlled Life *(Part 1)*

Your pain is probably going to be the worst thing you have ever experienced, and no one else would ever know or understand what you are going through. I want to share just what I went through with my eye so that you can have a perspective about what I am saying when I say that I know about pain. I also want to share about my eyes being opened (no pun intended) to the fact that what I was experiencing was not the worst thing that could happen to someone, though it felt like that at the time. God made sure that I had lots of people in my path who helped me understand that one simple fact.

It probably took two months for my eye to become really bad. Furthermore, I was just so busy living life that I forgot to take care of myself. As I mentioned in the previous chapter, I started this incredibly horrible and awesome episode of life with a trip to an eye doctor, who diagnosed me with *scleritis,* an inflammation of the white part of my eye. The sclera, the hardest structural part of the eye, is made of a cartilage-like substance. It would be similar to having terrible arthritis in the eye that hurts with every movement. The doctors were great and very thorough with me and had me take a relatively common treatment for my condition called a Prednisone burst. This is a four-day 40 mg oral dose that is used to try and obliterate the inflammation in a decisive and convincing manner. This did not work, and I was referred to one of the best ophthalmologists in the entire Denver area, Dr. Goldstein.

Again, I had great care and great people to work with but the same outcome. I was on massive doses of Advil, which helped a little, but the inflammation remained in my eye. So the doctor tried prednisone topical eye drops, which I needed to take three times a day. Due to the fact that eye drops can't absorb into the sclera, it didn't really help. There was one test performed on my eyes that I will never forget called gonioscopy. The doctor numbed my eye and then used a glass eye-piece, pressed onto the front of my eye, to look around the outer edges and tear duct of my eye. It was so bad that I felt as if I were losing my breath. Think about someone pushing on an arthritic joint.

The numbing drop did nothing for the deep, throbbing pain that coincided. Because I was out of work and at home, my cousin, Stephen, had picked me up and brought me to the eye doctor for that test. He sat in the waiting room and prayed for me during the entire process. I had so many visits to that office that I knew all the tech staff–and they knew me–by name. That is when you know you are a frequent visitor to the doctor. I received such great care from Dr. Goldstein and his team during this time. I know that his office and team were instrumental in helping me through that particular season of my journey, and I am forever indebted to them for the wonderful care they gave me.

During this time, when my eye was so inflamed, I felt as if I were going crazy from the pain in the entire left side of my head, and I was only getting about one or two hours of intermittent sleep every night as a result. The pain was a deep, throbbing headache that originated at the back of my eyeball. I would get up at 3:00 a.m. and take hot baths just to get my mind off of the pain. I would pull on my hair and the scalp below in an effort to alleviate the pain. I would go to the middle floor of our house and walk around in a circle and ask God, "Why?" for hours on end. Especially in the early years of being sick, I could not get over the fact that (in my mind) I felt I had not done anything to deserve this kind of pain. This was all going on while I was trying to be a youth pastor and to work with my high school students at the church, not to mention attempting to be the husband that Yolanda needed.

I remember the mental struggle I had each day, trying to stay focused on my ministry to the students while my physical situation got worse. I would take walks around the church building to get my mind off my situation and just to breathe some fresh air. I remember the day I came into my office and was looking at my computer screen when, all of a sudden, my left eye went blurry. No matter what I did to try to blink or rub the vision back, it couldn't be refocused. There was such an explosion of helplessness that went off in my mind and heart when this happened, and I instantly knew that what was happening with my eye was going to be a long lesson-learning situation.

After a conversation with my senior pastors, I agreed with them that I needed to step down as the youth pastor and let someone else take over. I can remember the fight in my mind and heart at that moment. My mind was acknowledging that I was sick and could not care for the students in the way I needed to, but my heart still wanted to be with them and help them grow. I truly loved each of those kids at Orchard Road and the time that Yolanda and I spent with them. From the first day I started working at the church, I can remember them asking Yolanda and me, about every six months, if we were going to be leaving. It took time to establish trust in them that we loved them and were not going anywhere. I can remember asking God how He could call me to this youth pastor position and yet not allow me to perform the tasks necessary for the teens? It was a very confusing time for me with God and the first time in my life that I was not sure if I could continue to trust Him. For some reason, I knew that God was still with me, but I didn't want to trust His power in my life. It wasn't that His power was unable to get me through my situation but rather that I was not willing to accept His strength at that time.

I then went on a twelve-week paid leave to allow my eye to get better. Meanwhile, Pastor Sarah Bowling and Pastor Jill Hilbrich ran the youth ministry for me. Remember when I said, at the beginning of this chapter, that pain is relative? Well to me, the pain I was going through became more important to me than anything that my youth students were going through. This was my life lesson about the priority that pain takes in a person's life. When people are sick or dealing with pain and act out in an anti-social, sometimes aggressive or rejecting, manner, I am not shocked anymore. I have a greater level of empathy for them because of what I went through. I am forever indebted to Jill and Sarah for helping out with the youth ministry while I was going through my situation. I loved those kids so much and wanted them to get the right kind of attention while I was out.

I knew it was a transition point in my life when I had to step down from youth ministry because of my eye. Even though I still loved my kids deeply, I soon realized I was no longer going to be a youth pastor. Because of the sickness I was facing, I knew my life was in for a drastic change. The mental pain, depression, and anguish came from not knowing WHAT that next step was going to be. I am not sure which is worse: knowing there is a next step but not knowing what it is or knowing what the next step is and not feeling adequate to do those things. Looking back, I now know and understand the trust that God was trying to build between Him and me. At the time though, I thought it was just more *crap* that He saw as *holy*.

I remember the day I came to the end of my care with my ophthalmologist at that time. Our youth were getting ready to go on a mission trip to Brazil. It had been planned and arranged for many months by Yolanda and my youth staff. I had done the recruitment for it, and I had every intention of leading the students on it. But at the doctor's office, the doctor told me that there was nothing else that he could do for me, and he sent me home. I knew that I was not going to be able to go on the mission trip with my students because of the condition of my eye. I was with Yolanda and just looked at her and asked what was going to happen to me. It was one of the darkest hours of my life.

Holy Crap Moment

If you are in a place of despair because of something going on in your life, please know that Jesus cares for you; don't give up. Even as I type this section, I am praying for your hope to be sustained as you read these words. See. There IS someone praying for you in your situation and believing you are going to make it!!

Take a Moment

_____

_____

_____

_____

I knew that people were praying for me, but I couldn't even pray for myself. All those years in Royal Rangers at church (Christian Boy Scouts), all the years on the Bible Quiz team, all those Wednesday nights growing up during high school of leading worship for the youth group, four and a half years earning two Bible college degrees, ten years and four churches of leading youth ministry, and I couldn't even say the name of Jesus. As I think back, that is probably a harder realization than even the pain I was going through at that point. All those years of doing "good Jesus stuff," and I couldn't even say His name. You may ask, "Brian, why are you telling me this? I thought this was a book to show me that all I need to say is 'Jesus' and everything is taken care of." I am not discounting the power of the name of Jesus, but I am saying that I realized from my pain, during those years, that I didn't really know who Jesus was. I could read about Him, sing about Him, and even preach about Him, but I didn't *know* Him.

Holy Crap Moment:

I want to challenge you to not wait for an "eye experience" in your life. Get to know Jesus and how much He loves you and wants you to be an overcomer in life. Start by reaching out to God even if it's something a little like, "God, I need your help and don't know how to trust You. Please put people in my life to help show me how."

Take a Moment

_____

_____

_____

_____

I also want you to know that, even though I couldn't pray, I knew there were people praying for me and lifting me up when I couldn't lift myself up. That was not because I was living a lone ranger life but because I had a church home where people prayed for me and encouraged me when I would rather have told them to leave me alone. I never believed it before I got sick, but I do think there are times in a Christian person's life when you need "spiritual life-support."

Spiritual life-support functions in the same way medical life-support functions for a person, physically. It is support that enables your vital functions to continue to operate. But just as a person cannot stay on physical life-support forever, neither can a person stay on spiritual life-support forever. I think these are times in your life when you cannot pray prayers for yourself or "stand on that scripture" (to use that good Charismatic Christian expression) enough to see your breakthrough. As I have said, this is not saying that I didn't believe in God or His role in my life, but I knew, when I was sick, that I could not do the "Christian things" to overcome, and I needed some help. There would come a point when I started to stand on my own, but when I wasn't there yet, it felt amazing knowing that others were standing in the gap and praying for me in ways I could not pray for myself.

Holy Crap Moment:

If you don't have a good Jesus-focused, Bible-believing church to call home, then you need to find one. I know that the only way I was able to make it through my painful situation in life was through the support and prayers of the people at Orchard Road Christian Center and other churches of which Yolanda and I had been a part. I know this sounds old-fashioned in today's "church is uncool" society, but I don't have a better solution for you—because you WILL need support when crap happens in life.

Take a Moment

_____

_____

_____

_____

At the end of that horrendous day, my eye doctor called me and said that he had a specialist he wanted me to see. Just when I was ready to give up, God came through in the form of a reason to hang on just one more day and believe that this nightmare would be over. I would love to tell you that I had a God moment and realized His hand in the situation, but I didn't. I thought, "Well, maybe I can buy some more time and keep my eye for a bit longer."

After the twelve weeks of being on sick leave from the church, I knew it was time to step aside and let the church hire someone else to take my place. I was then out of full-time church work for about eleven months, but I was doing odd jobs and working at a home theater installation company. I appreciate the time my boss, Scott, let me work there, and it was another instrumental time in my life. I was growing up and realizing what it was like to be outside of the church walls as an adult and have to make an income. Until I got sick, I had spent my entire adult, post-college life inside the four walls of a church, always doing ministry. The time I worked for Scott helped me understand the expectations I had put on my volunteers to work their forty-hour-a-week jobs and then come to church and give me 100 percent. It helped me understand just how great my leadership team was, and I can say thank you with a new understanding of what they gave to the students of Orchard Road for the years I was over the high school ministry. This was one of many lessons God was teaching me by removing me from church ministry and letting my eye become a liability to my future–or so I thought. Dr. Goldstein was an amazing ophthalmologist but had the same answers as the rest of the doctors who had seen me. It was time for the next chapter of my life story.

I started going to the Lion's Eye Institute of Colorado University, which is a research center for eye diseases. My new medical family, Dr. Mandava and his team at the clinic, were wonderful in helping to do what they could to treat my condition with excellence and professionalism. Whenever Yolanda and I would go for an appointment, it was helpful that I felt as if we were among family who had my best interests in mind, even though those were the hardest years of my life. I went there for about three and a half years of the four and a half that I was sick, and I know now that God had a greater plan for everything I went through by placing me there. The first thing the doctor ordered for me was a fluorescein angiography. This is where they inject dye into your blood stream and see how the blood flows through the different layers of the retina, which is the brain tissue part of the eye that allows you to see. Many eye diseases can be diagnosed with this procedure.

Now, there is a side story of craziness connected to this procedure, which added further madness to what I was already going through with my eye. The eye clinic had me sign a waiver saying that the hospital was not responsible if I had an adverse reaction to the dye injected into my bloodstream. This adverse reaction could be anything from a simple rash to nausea to a one in twenty-five thousand chance of anaphylaxis, which is a life-threatening allergic reaction. That is enough to say "Holy Crap" right there! I have had this procedure done twice, and, both times, my eye results came back inconclusive. The sad thing was that by the time I had the second procedure, I didn't really even care if I was the one who had an allergic response and died. As I look back on that time in my life, it seemed to be a normal response to what was going on with me, but what a selfish way of thinking! I will expand more on this in a later chapter about how pain can cause you to be very selfish. (That was not a very fun chapter to write, by the way.)

I also had a scan that measured the thickness of the retina to see if there were any minute abnormalities in the retinal tissues, which could have been a sign of growths or cancer growing in the back of my eye. But the procedure I looked forward to the least was one I had at least four times, and it was an ultrasound of my eye. In this procedure, I was to look as far right as I could, and the doctor would put a jelly on the end of a sensor and then push the sensor onto the surface of my eye–and yes, this is as uncomfortable as it sounds. It was really the best way to get comparative pictures of the activity in my eye and to see the level of damage occurring.

After these tests, I started medical treatment for my eye condition that every doctor confirmed I had, but no one could tell me what caused it. This doctor started me on 80 mg of oral prednisone a day to help stop the inflammation. Because prednisone is so detrimental to a person's system, doctors like to administer it one dose per day so the body has time to recover and to give the kidneys and liver a rest from such an intensely toxic drug in the body. The problem is that my eye would be fine for about eighteen hours, and then the last six hours of the day it would get red and painful again.

I can remember going to the eye doctor about every other day because there were changes happening so fast in my eye that I could actually watch what seemed like my retina detaching from the back of my eye because of the inflammation. After about two weeks, we finally got the dosage right. I was taking two oral doses of 40 mg of this heavy drug every day for about six months. This regimen continued for the next four and a half years: taking drugs at 9:00 a.m. and 9:00 p.m. *every* day. My eye started to improve, but no one can be on that dose of prednisone for any length of time and stay healthy, so I started to take other drugs to work symbiotically with it. This was in an effort to wean me off the prednisone. That was the hope, anyway. I didn't have the normal side effects initially from taking prednisone but eventually had the sleepless nights, weight gain, and restlessness that come with the drug.

I started with Methotrexate, which is a drug to help people who have arthritis or other inflammatory diseases. Now, I have to tell you something. Before I got sick, the worst thing I could think of was going to the dentist, getting my eyes dilated, or having any kind of needle stuck anywhere in my body. Discounting the dentist trips, I have had my eyes dilated well over 200 times, complete with blurred vision at shorter distances and photosensitivity afterwards. I feel sure I gave what seems like gallons of blood, for every reason, and had more needles pushed into me than a pin cushion at a seamstress's convention. I actually had to learn to give myself shots of Methotrexate in the leg. This was very strange for me since I hated needles and was inflicting this pain on myself on purpose. It was as if I was living a nightmare every time I would put that needle in my leg. I can remember trying to pray, "God, I thank you that this drug is only doing what it is supposed to do and not harming other parts or anything else in my body." I remember being so depressed while I was sitting alone in my house, Yolanda not there, sticking that needle in my leg day after day, over and over and over again.

Chapter 5

Overcoming a Pain-Controlled Life *(Part 2)*

When medical treatments for my eye began, so did bouts of depression and thoughts of killing myself. I cannot tell you why, but from 2:30 p.m. until about 5:00 p.m. in the afternoon on weekdays was the hardest time of day for me. Yolanda was at work, trying to make enough money to pay our bills, and I was home alone all day. Now that I can reflect on my situation, I felt as if I were losing my liberties, which included being able to drive. Now, for a kid from Montana (the wide-open, Big Sky state) who was able to drive when he was fifteen, that was something I was fighting against with all my might.

When I was sick and at home, I developed regimens during the day. I would get in my truck, drive to the grocery store, and just buy one thing, like an orange or a banana–just for something to do. I would always use the self-checkout and use the keypad to find the item in the list of produce in the computer just so it would take longer to check out. This may seem strange, but I was doing things to try to hold onto the normalcy of being able to drive. I also thought that if I was going to go blind, I wanted to do as much driving as I could before the doctor told me I couldn't. The fact is that with a doctor's note, I would be safe to drive even with one eye, but at the time the devil was just bringing additional lies to my mind, bringing me deeper into depression.

These times in my mind were so dark for me; I felt very helpless. One day, I told Yolanda that I wanted her to get the gun and hide it from me because of the suicidal thoughts I was having. I cannot think of a darker time, mentally, for me. I was filled with so much doubt about my future and the condition of my life. I didn't have enough mental power in my brain to deal with the stresses and the concerns that dominated my thinking. It also made me flash back to the times when I had teens or adults in my office who were dealing with levels of depression, and I told them to just trust God more. I can't beat myself up for saying those things because that is all I knew then. However, now that I have experience with what it means to have depression, those words will never ever come out of my mouth again.

Holy Crap Moment:

If you are someone who works with or counsels people, please be careful with ultimatums you put on them. I am not saying that an expectation of change in their actions is wrong when working with people who need changes in their lives, but an attitude of "do these five things and then we will talk" is not constructive. Today, get better at listening and get worse at telling people what to do. If you are a follower of Christ, let God bring the changes people need to see, and then be there to help them walk those principles out in their lives.

Take a Moment

_____

_____

_____

_____

I actually had some counseling around this time, as well, for which the church paid. I really think this was a great help to me, in retrospect. It helped me to deal with my thoughts and to really categorize them into smaller bits, so I could control them. I am not against professional counseling if you feel like you need it. I really think there is the spiritual side to who we are, and then there is the personal discipline side to us that sometimes needs help. My view is that we would not need counseling if God did not give us a free will to make decisions that cause us to turn away from Him. God provides all the necessary tools for us to be able to make the right decisions, but counseling can help us line up our free will with God's ability to bring good change to our lives.

Okay, back to the medical story. Needless to say, the Methotrexate did not work, just as nothing else I took did. The doctor came to the conclusion that the normal causes were all ruled out and the more rare diseases should be considered. So we were advised to get a kidney biopsy to check for Wegener's granulomatosis. I thought this was good because if they found out it was Wegener's granulomatosis, then I could know what the root of the disease was and get treatment. What my wonderful wife strategically forgot to inform me of was that it is an incurable disease. Now that I know this information, I sure am glad I didn't know then about the problems associated with it, or that would have been the cherry on top of the iced turd cake I was "enjoying."

Holy Crap Moment

Thinking back now about my story, I can remember the doctors telling me that I didn't have some inoperable disease. I think even now about people who have been diagnosed with one, and my heart goes out to you. It inspires me to pray for your healing and believe for God's best in your life even now. To me, it is SO IMPORTANT to focus on the cup as half-full instead of half-empty.

Sometimes, these thoughts are enough to at least get you through the day—and when you are sick, that is a premium. What is one positive (maybe in a sea of negatives) that you can focus on in your situation?

Take a Moment

_____

_____

_____

_____

I was sent to the hospital for three days and had a large hook-like needle stuck in my back so the doctors could get a sample of my kidney. I remember singing with Yolanda, *"He didn't lift us up to let us down"* a Christian song from when I grew up while we waited in the doctor's office for me to be admitted to the hospital. This was a very weird time for me emotionally.

For three days, I was in ICU for observation to make sure there was no internal bleeding from the kidney procedure. During this time, even though I was in an emotionally shell-shocked state, I can remember talking to a couple of nurses about my story and my relationship with Jesus. I can also remember walking around the hospital and seeing the rows of chairs in the dialysis room and the cancer treatment area full of people dealing with far greater things than my pain and eye condition. I do believe my story can have a greater impact on those of you who are not associated with church because being a pastor or a good person neither exempted me from experiencing pain in life nor did it prepare me. My entire eyeball time has really opened my eyes to the fact that neither good works nor good intentions have anything to do with keeping pain out of your life.

Holy Crap Moment:

We can live in a false sense of security in life. We can think that there are things in our lives that we can do to exempt ourselves from having to deal with pain. When we stop thinking we are impervious to painful situations, we begin to see the need for God in our lives and for a greater trust in Him than on our own power.

Take a Moment

_____

_____

_____

_____

I guess you could say that, at that time in my experience, if I were given an opportunity to witness to someone or tell them about my situation, I could quite easily do it, but if it came to me having a conversation with God, I would have some issues. I was in a strange place of being able to share with others about Jesus while my personal relationship with Him was filled with anger and distrust in His ways. I wanted to know why this was happening and how I was going to get out of my situation without having to go through the patient process of revelation.

The kidney biopsy came back negative, which was good, but the doctors decided that I needed to get a CT scan and an MRI to check for additional rare issues that could cause my eye to be perpetually and dangerously inflamed. I can remember when I checked out of the hospital and Yolanda and I went home to sit and wait for the results of the MRI. We were both concerned I might have some kind of eye cancer. I know what it's like to be home, everything eerily peaceful and quiet, while waiting for test results to come from the doctor and expecting the worst, not the best. I know the depth of worry and mind games the devil can play with you when you are dealing with the unknown.

I remember very clearly the phone call from the doctor. Yolanda answered the phone, had the conversation with the doctor, and heard that everything was fine. She began to cry when she told me the results. It was the oddest feeling of relief and yet confusion that I have ever experienced in my life. It was the close to another episode of "find out something else that is not wrong with your eye, but we still don't know the reason it is flaring up." The emotional strain of nobody knowing what was wrong with me made the unceasing and excruciating physical experience that much more traumatic.

In a previous chapter, I talked about how the devil works in two specific areas: the *unknown* and the *alone*. This moment was a perfect example of those lonely and desolate times when he was working in both. After no success with the kidney biopsy, I went back to the eye doctor, and we decided to start Imuran. At one point, I was going to the doctor about two to three times a week to get my eye dilated and checked. My eye would change, sometimes by the hour, and I could actually see flashes of fluid moving around in my eye as it was deteriorating while I was lying in bed in the middle of the night.

There were many nights when I would have a flashlight in the dark while lying in bed, and I would turn the flashlight on, open my bad eye, and try to see if my eye was any better than it had been five minutes before and how much damage was occurring. This frequency was not an exaggeration and is a telling example of the depth of worry and despair I existed in. I would do this sometimes fifty times or more per night. Yolanda would tell me to shut the light off, but I wanted to see if my eye was getting worse or getting better, and it seemed as if it was always getting worse. In retrospect, it would have been better for me to not keep looking for a worsening condition but to keep expecting an improving condition. The damage was so bad that I actually had some of the layers of the retina detaching from each other because of the inflammation as a result of my immune system attacking my eye.

An overactive immune system, also called autoimmune, was the best diagnosis the doctors could give me about my body and what was happening with my eye. That was why I started taking Imuran, which is primarily a drug that patients take so the body doesn't attack transplant organs. I didn't have a transplant organ, but the doctors thought this would work because it might help stop the over-activity of my immune system. In doing a study about the drug for this book, one of the side effects of Imuran was that it can actually CAUSE cancer! Even after all the years of being off these drugs, that is disturbing to think about all the drugs that went through my body for those four and a half years.

During this time of being on so many medications and working with the medical world, I was also being seen by and working with naturopaths. My aunt Sharon was amazing for everything she did for Yolanda and me and connecting us with her naturopath. I do think that the time I spent working with the doctors, naturopaths, friends, and family was all a part of me being here today.

So I bet you will never guess what happened with Imuran. Yep, it didn't work either. I was trying to get off of the prednisone through all of this, so each time a drug did not work for me, it caused me to have to increase the prednisone from about 20 mg back up to 40-50 mg per dose, two times a day, every time. This was all part of the emotional tearing that occurred in me each time I had to go back up on the prednisone. Each time that happened, it would be another reason to disbelieve that I would *ever* be off of prednisone, and there was definitely a war going on in my head each time I would have a drug not work and have to increase my prednisone. That was really my watermark as to how I was doing with my eye and whether or not I had any faith in the truths of the Bible or anything anyone was praying for me. These were more reasons to realize how important the people really were who were praying for me in this season of life.

Prednisone itself is really an amazing drug in both a good and a bad way. It has the ability to work instantly but with wicked after-effects in your body, including kidney problems, liver problems, and a vast array of chronic post-treatment issues that essentially affect every part of the human body. I remember going to the dentist, and when he looked at my teeth, he said my gums looked great (because of the prednisone) but my teeth had lost some bone mass (because of the prednisone). That is why the doctors did not want me to be on it for very long, because of the damage it was doing to my insides.

At one point, because of the drugs I was on, I had lost 28 percent of my bone mass, which is not good. I was six feet six inches tall and actually lost some of that height. Once the doctors learned that my bone mass was dropping, they put me on Fosamax to counteract the effects of the prednisone. If your bone mass drops too low, then you have a greater possibility of developing osteoporosis or brittle bones and not being able to heal well if you have a break of any kind.

Because the Imuran treatment was not working, I was prescribed more powerful immune-suppressive drugs, and I was running out of options. Remicade was the next drug of choice. This was an actual IV drip that I would go into a clinic to receive once a month. I would arrive at the Arthritis Clinic, which was monitoring the drugs and toxicity in my system, and sit in a "sick room" for three hours once a month. Remicade was another one of those drugs that caused me to think, "Is this really happening to me?" Before I got sick, I never took any pills and was basically in pretty good health. If I had a headache, I would go lie down for an hour and then be as good as new.

At the clinic, I sat and talked with a girl of about nineteen years of age who had to come in monthly to receive treatment for a disease that doctors said could not be cured, only managed. I sat and talked with people who had Lupus and other diseases that could only be managed by Remicade. It was an introduction into a community of people I was privileged to spend time with and learn from by hearing their stories of dealing with diseases that they had had for years and years. I can also remember countless trips at all times of day to Walgreens to stand in line with people like me who were also picking up drugs and who had to make waiting in that line and sticking to a regimen of medication a part of their lifestyle, too. I know that God let me see a glimpse of what people deal with every day of their lives, both emotionally and physically.

The Bible is replete with examples in Matthew about how Jesus had compassion on people and then interacted with them and helped them in some way. I know that one of the positives that came from being in that sick room and seeing people around me who were sicker than I was that I learned about the compassion Jesus had for people. It was like He felt their pain and could see the need before He met the need in people. Being sick for all those years, I had wonderful (though it seemed like crap at the time) opportunities to see how people live with a disease that affects all areas of their lives, including the emotional, financial, and physical aspects.

The Remicade treatments were $6,000 per visit, and I had to be approved on a grant list to have the cost of this covered. I was also accumulating doctor bills like bubble gum trading cards. I can remember when we were receiving a medical bill in the mail EVERY DAY from all the doctors and specialists who were seeing me. After about nine months of IV treatments, the doctor evaluated me again, and, unbelievably, the drugs were not working. So I was put on one last drug.

Sometime in the next few weeks, my doctor and I decided I needed to be seen by another specialist at Barnes Eye Institute in St. Louis, Missouri, to see if he could help me as well. The interaction I had with people on these trips was awesome. The perspective I got from talking to others going through crap that I could only imagine (and not in a good Christian song kind of way) changed my life.

Yolanda and I stayed with an uncle-in-law I had never met whose wife was dealing with cancer. That was another wonderful time for "poor ol' Bri and his rotting eye" to have a reality check and understand that his pain was not the worst thing in mankind's history to happen to someone. My aunt and uncle opened their home to Yolanda and me and shuttled us around town. It was an act of kindness I will never forget. They are a wonderful couple, and we appreciated staying with them while we were there. We also had a couple from my church, Jim and JoAnn Caswell, who were in St. Louis and came to the hospital where we were to pray with and encourage us. These were more church people who helped us keep our heads above water when we felt, in many ways, as if we were sinking in despair.

The eye specialist looked at my eye, and then we had a conversation I will never forget. He told me that there was a lot of damage in my eye, and he was recommending that I go on Cytoxan. This is a retired chemotherapeutic drug that was used for people with cancer. This drug can cause bladder cancer if taken for too long without enough consistent hydration. Plus, I had enough common knowledge that a drug with the word "tox" in it was probably not good for you. I will never forget what he said after he made his evaluation. He talked to me about removing my eye and trying to save the body as a priority – and that perhaps I should allow the eye to be removed.

Before my St. Louis trip, I had a few conversations with my eye doctor back home about this, but it never really sank in until that moment. It wasn't like I started crying. It was more like a sick feeling in my stomach that wouldn't go away. I became flushed and felt some of the blood leave my face as I sat in the darkened exam room. I came face-to-face with the true nature of the devil and one of his main tools of destruction, fear. I had preached great sermons about combating the power of fear that the devil uses to keep people in check with the pain in life. I think back now about that moment, and I do not want to ever feel as helpless as I did then. I am now focused on the power inside of me through Christ versus the powers that come against me in life that want to steal my joy and rob me of mental peace.

When I got back to Denver, I went ahead and started almost two years of Cytoxan treatments. During that time, I went to a National Day of Healing prayer meeting at our church. My wife and I believe that was the beginning of the healing in my body. I was eventually able to get off all prednisone and also get off the Cytoxan. As I am typing this, my eye has been medically cleared for about six years now. It has been a slow, difficult process to write this book and not have flashbacks and old worries creep in and distract my current life. Looking back, though, I can see God's hand in everything I went through and that each phase of life, each drug, and each doctor I interacted with had a purpose that was greater than my current circumstance.

Through the four-and-a-half years of my eye condition, I was seen by about twenty-seven doctors and residents, including five naturopaths, an infectious disease doctor (who gave me back my co-pay and told me that I didn't even need to be in his office), an allergist, and probably the best ophthalmologist and vitro-retinal eye disease doctor this side of the Mississippi. All of them have confirmed that I had scleritis, but none of them knew what caused it.

Now comes all the good stuff, including the things I believe God has shown me through these four-and-a-half years of self-discovery. Strap on your seat belt, because we are just getting started.

Chapter 6

Healing - The Lifestyle Modifier

I have really had my eyes opened these past few years to what it means to be sick and how it changes your life. Until a few years ago, the worst thing medically I had to deal with was getting a headache or the flu. I would sleep it off or stay in bed for a few days until it passed. I wouldn't even take aspirin for a headache or any kind of pill for anything, but for about three years when I was sick, I was taking up to thirty pills per day. While I had my eye condition, there were vacations I couldn't take, regimented medication times I had to adhere to, foods I needed to stay away from, emotional stress from worrying about the future, and a change in my attitude toward people and being around people.

I knew people loved me, but I just didn't want them to ask about my eye or about anything that had been going on with me physically. That was probably the weirdest thing about what happened to me when I got sick: I didn't want to be around or communicate in any way with human beings. I was so consumed with how I felt and the worry of going blind or dying that I pushed everyone away from me, and it was not pretty. I was even mean to our dog, Wilson, and I actually can't believe he even still liked me after so many days and nights of my being mean to him. If anyone knows me, they know I love people and would rather be around lots of people than be by myself any day of the week. When I think back on being sick, it still blows my mind to think I was the guy who didn't want to leave the house for about four months.

One night, Yolanda didn't want to cook, and she wanted to drive up the street to a restaurant about six blocks from our house. She told me, "Brian, we are still married, and I want to go eat dinner with my husband." I remember the terror going through my mind and body as I put on nicer clothes to leave the house and drive in the car up the street to be stared at by the waitress and the people sitting in the booths around me. Of course, it was silly to think that way, but the devil has a way of taking a seed of any pain or fear and growing a redwood out of it.

Holy Crap Moment:

What are you worried about right now in your life that has a hold on you to the point of paralysis? Take a Moment to think about what is causing that terror in your mind. It may be time to turn to God and ask Him to help you with your mind. I am not saying that you will be immune to pain in life when God is in control, but you will have Him to be able to help you walk through your situation.

Take a Moment

_____

_____

_____

_____

Your lifestyle can be changed by many things. Even though my specific disease was a physical pain, I was mentally trapped into thinking things were worse than they really were. I thought my life was slowly ending and that the disease that was eating my eye would eventually kill me. I also thought that going blind was the absolute worst way to have to exist on this earth. It is interesting for me to look back on my life, these past few years, and see the connection between my physical state and my emotional state and how each one affected the other.

You may be dealing with a type of mental pain in your life, and it is also affecting your lifestyle. Sometimes the mental side of pain is worse than the physical. Even if the doctors needed to remove my eye, or if I were to go blind, the mental anguish of what I was dealing with could take years or even a lifetime to get over. I never understood depression and the feeling of wanting to commit suicide until I was the one considering getting the gun. That would have been the ultimate change of lifestyle–death!

I was not only affecting myself personally; I was completely oblivious to how my actions from being sick were affecting my relationship and lifestyle with my wife, Yolanda. I was always too sick to even go out to eat or really to go anywhere in public that didn't have to do with a doctor visit or too mentally preoccupied with my condition to remember what it was like to laugh, and I pushed her away in many ways. For me to say that I forgot what it was like to laugh is a huge statement for anyone who has known me longer than a few minutes.

I knew Yolanda loved me, but I didn't want to hear the scriptures she wanted me to speak, and I didn't want to pray with her. So she would stay up and pace around my bed and pray for me until I fell asleep, at the point when I was only getting a few minutes of sleep each night because of the pain. All of these things were affecting my lifestyle, not only with my family and friends but also my lifestyle with God. I was realizing things about my relationship with God that I didn't like. What I am saying is that when we go through times of pain, it can affect everything around us, including the ones we love.

Holy Crap Moment

If you are dealing with some kind of pain in your life, think of the people in your life that you are affecting. I know this will be hard, but realize that, when you are difficult with the people around you who love you, you are allowing the things that are affecting you to affect others too. Today, ask God to help you with your attitude in the middle of your storm.

Take a Moment

_____

_____

_____

_____

My lifestyle and the things I really enjoyed doing were severely affected by my pain. I was more than just sad that I couldn't go on the Brazil mission trip with my youth group when my eye was so bad and painful that I would rather try to sleep than walk around the house. Those months and years of having to take medication at certain times of the day certainly dominated and affected when I could eat lunch or dinner, too. Even now, at 9:00 a.m. and 9:00 p.m., it triggers my memory of taking the prednisone that was supposed to be helping the inflammation in my left eye but gave me a bubble of fluid called central serous under my retina in my good eye instead.

One night, when my eye was so bad that I could actually see the fluid flashing in my left eye and the retina becoming partially detached, I thought, "This is it. You will have a glass eye and may go completely blind and never have a job again and Yolanda will leave you and you might as well kill yourself." For you grammatical all-stars reading this, I intended the last sentence to be run-on because that's how the devil works–stringing thoughts together so that you can't emotionally breathe and using compounded mental worry to affect your physical life. My sickness changed the plans that I had for my life and was a catalyst for fear that actually changed my attitude and interaction with people, my God, my family, and my wife–kind of a problem when you are a pastor, a son, a brother, a husband–and the main requirement of your job is to connect with and talk to people.

Now you are probably wondering why I just wrote about all this pain and worry when the title of this chapter has to do with healing. Remember this: to understand healing for a person, you need to understand the pain he or she goes through. I do think this understanding can be God-given because you can pray for someone who is going through something without having gone through it yourself. But I also think that, when you have gone through something mentally, emotionally, or physically severe, you have a reference for what it means to ask God for healing in someone's life.

You are not just asking for a person to be healed of a broken heart, a deep emotional wound, or any number of physical ailments; you are asking for his or her lifestyle to change. You are asking for him to be able to go on vacations he loves, to be freed from being inconveniently tied to taking drugs, to be able to eat foods again he was not able to eat, or to be mentally free from something that has possibly had him tied down for years. You are asking for his or her marriage to improve and his or her outlook on life to change dramatically. Now, when I pray for someone to be healed, no matter what it is, I am asking God to change that person's life, not just his circumstances.

Holy Crap Moment:

Take about five minutes right now and ask God to help someone you know who is going through a struggle emotionally, physically, or maybe spiritually. The best times to ask God to help others are when you are in need yourself. Talk to God from a position at which you understand the level of desperation that others may be in. It will start to change your perspective and what you are currently going through.

Take a Moment

_____

_____

_____

_____

When I realized I was praying for a lifestyle change for people, I no longer said, "I will be praying for you" without understanding the full implications of that statement. I was making a commitment to them. One of the keys for a person's healthy lifestyle is a connection to a church body. I think the church, in general, uses a lot of religious or trite "yes, brother/sister, I will be praying for you" sayings that have pushed more people away than they have attracted. I am not giving a pass to the people who have walked away from a physical church or the church body in general, but when you have people in the church say, "I will be praying for you," for example, and they don't actually do it, people know, get hurt, and sometimes leave. How do you know when someone really loves you? They prove the things that come out of their mouths by their obvious actions.

I was reading the Bible in the book of Matthew where it says *Jesus had compassion on them...and then He healed them.* That verse stuck out so vividly when I was sick because I realize now it was emphasizing that Jesus not only felt compassion for them but I think He also saw the change that was going to come to their lives when they were healed. People would come to Jesus all the time with things they WANTED, but He would also give them the things they NEEDED. We need to realize that God sees multiple steps in front of us and when He sees us hurting, He has compassion on us.

Now, if you are still in the middle of the crap in your life and you're saying, "Then why isn't God healing me?" I can't answer this question except to say that the Bible says that He heals all of our diseases and that He took our infirmities. In other books like this one, you may have someone trying to explain why bad things happen to good people, but I cannot say I have the answer to that question. I'm sorry if you picked up this book expecting all your questions to be answered. All I can do is share my personal experience and what I felt that God showed me. Hopefully, there is something in this book that might be able to help you hang on just one more day or help you rekindle a relationship with God that was once there and has died out. I think, sometimes, we live life angry at God and we waste days thinking that our negative attitude has really taught God a lesson. Trying to answer questions that may never have an answer is a sure-fire way to ruin other areas of our lives and possibly keep us from healthy, functioning relationships.

Being healed brings lifestyle changes, and we need to plan on walking away changed from who we were before we got sick, had a child fall ill, had our heart crushed, or felt betrayed by a church body. If we are not healed and are still wondering why, then I think we need to learn to ask the right question when things don't change. Instead of asking *why*, maybe we should be asking *what* we need to know about the true nature of God that would help us against this sickness or painful situation—primarily, that He wants me well and strong, emotionally and physically.

Holy Crap Moment:

Right now, take a minute and instead of asking God, "Why am I going through this?" ask Him, "What do I need to know about You in order to overcome this pain/sickness?" Your perspective in ANY situation will determine your ability to make healthy, non-reactive decisions that will ultimately determine your destiny.

Take a Moment

_____

_____

_____

_____

Sometimes in life all we have is hope. I know that sounds like a cliché, but it is something I dealt with for almost five years. My hope came from a focus on the Bible and the power of its words, even when I was wrestling with my personal relationship with God. Biblical hope is solid and means confident expectation of good. This is not a Hail Mary kind of doubtful wishing, which is what some people have in life to get them through. The Bible is full of the confident expectation kind of hope, but here are a couple of verses that speak about hope in the lives of those who consider God their Leader in life. It says in Isaiah 49:23 that those who hope in God will never be disappointed or let down. Romans 5:5 says "And character [of this sort] produces [the habit of] joyful and confident hope...Such hope never disappoints or deludes or shames us, for God's love has been poured out in our hearts through the Holy Spirit who has been given to us"[8]

This kind of hope has never let me down through the years and is available to anyone who asks God for it.

Maybe the situation you are in will so shape you that you will be used to help other people get through difficult times when they have lost a loved one or have a child with a terminal illness. Maybe it's so that you can realize that the life we live is only a short breath when compared to eternity, and that is where God wants our focus. I cannot explain why God does not move when we think He should, but I can say this: if I believe that He created me for a greater purpose on this earth than for my physical comfort, then I can believe that how I feel is not as important as what I learn from the pains of life that are inevitable. I can believe that how I feel is not as important as my usefulness to others when I deal with that pain in life. God does not cause the pains and discomfort of life but that I

---

[8] Amplified (AMP) Bible

will do my part to believe He has everything under control because I cannot see the beginning of my life or the end.

The lifestyle change we are essentially asking for ourselves needs to come with a new game plan that will include us being a better person on the other side of our sickness or our pain. I also think this includes an obligation to share our stories with the people around us to help them get through a difficult time in their lives or prepare them for what it takes to, as the Bible says, "walk through the fire and not get burned"[9]

This book is a way of changing my small part of the world. I know there are people in my life who need to read this in order to be encouraged and maybe even to come back to Jesus, if they have been hurt in some way. I am grateful to God for a restoration of my lifestyle, and for the story I now have to change the world. My passion is to help people love God and not give up in the middle of possibly the worst time of their lives. My website, HolyCrapBook.com, is meant to revitalize your courage and fortify you along life's journey. I invite you to go there now and maybe just tell me your feelings after reading this section, or find a post there that can lift you up today!

---

[9] Isa 43:2 (NIV)

Chapter 7

Pain Pitfalls

There are certain things that come to mind when you deal with pain, but a pitfall is not usually one of them. A pitfall can be described as an unexpected, unforeseen, or surprising difficulty. The kinds of things that come to mind when I think of the pain I went through are self-pity, hopelessness, despair, thoughts of suicide, physical pain, etc. The list is just too great to count. I want to discuss in this chapter the things you never thought would ever happen when you get sick or when you go through any type of pain. To me, this chapter has some of the best gold in this book because now that I have gone through the worst part of being sick, I've had to climb out of some pitfalls, and I've learned how to avoid others. I think you will find these suggestions or nuggets quite interesting.

The pitfalls I mention in this chapter are not universal and can be different for every person dealing with pain. If you feel like you are on the other side of things like this, then great. But as I share these personal issues that I have dealt with and am still dealing with, I believe you'll find something in the next few pages which you can relate to as well, and maybe you can look at some of the pitfalls people get caught in with pain.

The first pitfall I want to discuss is spiritual expectation. You may hear "expectation" and say, "That's not a bad thing." I am talking about the kind of expectation, however, that says, "because I experienced pain, I expect God to come through and make up for

73

the pain He allowed me to go through" or "I want Him to come in and change my situation." The correct kind of expectation is seen in Psalms 5:3 where David is talking about himself rising in the morning, speaking to God, and then waiting in expectation. In some translations, it says, "I will look up." But the kind of negative expectation I am talking about has a certain depth of selfishness to it that I experienced and still confront to this day. This can be seen when I pray and expect God to do something about the problems I am experiencing *as though He owes it to me*. I am essentially asking God to come into my circumstances and change them to the way in which I have asked Him. I don't know why many of us in church have been taught and raised to selfishly believe that if we pray just the correct way, God will swoop in, *on our timing*, and save the day.

I really believe we need to have a new revelation about what it means to pray and have a conversation with God. The best way I can explain this is to compare it to a conversation in the physical realm. When I have a conversation with a friend, I have a different expectation than when I talk to someone in my family. I wouldn't necessarily ask some things of a friend, but I feel freer to ask openly of my family. That being said, it is unfair to think that a family member should do everything for me just because I asked. Why do we think that a conversation with God is any different? When I talk with my dad about something related to my car, I am asking him what he thinks would be best because I trust his judgment, and I know that he wants to take care of me. He is the professional at fixing cars, and I am the one who needs the information he has. I can still ask the question, but I need to trust that the answer he gives, even if I don't like it, is for my own good. I truly believe that our misinterpretation of prayer comes from a lack of trust in God.

Holy Crap Moment

Take some time right now and list three or four ways that you could do better at trusting God. If we start to identify the areas that are challenges for us, then we can begin to work on them and start to trust Him more.

Take a Moment

_____

_____

_____

_____

When we go through pain and ask for *our* will to be done in life, we are saying, "God, I love You and need an answer to this problem, but I don't trust in your timing nor do I believe that everything I go through in life is beneficial for me as long as I keep my eyes on You." The fundamental flaw with our will versus God's will is *our* way, which is a flawed, limited knowledge of our immediate surroundings, compared to God's will, which is limitless in its scope and operates on our behalf even when we experience crap in life. So this is what we do: we continue to think that if we ask the right way or frequently enough, God is going to change His plan based on our immediate discomfort. Then we say that God is not listening to us because we can't take a *no* or a *wait* from Him.

I was asking God to heal me because I had received some of the best Sunday school teaching, Bible college education, and life experiences in youth ministry that anyone ever had. I thought that because I was good my whole life–in the world's eyes–that I should not have to deal with the possibility of losing my eye, going blind, or even dying if it turned out to be something cancerous. The problem with that logic is my "greatest awesomeness" as a human being was still dirty, filthy rags in God's sight.[10] I needed to see that God's healing was available to me, not because I was "all that" and I deserved it, but purely on the merit of His own goodness and grace.

I never really understood what that meant until I felt as if God was treating me like the rest of the world, who were not as "holy and righteous" as I was, or so I thought. If you are someone who has asked Jesus to be the Leader of your life, but you've possibly done everything wrong and evil by the world's standards in your past, you are still worthy to pray and be heard by the Creator of the universe. I can tell you that you cannot blame your circumstances on the evil that you have done. There are things we do in life that have consequences, but if Jesus is your Leader, God is not keeping a record in heaven of all the evil things you have ever done. Neither is He keeping a merit badge wall of the good things you have done in life. The key is knowing that

> If you are someone who has asked Jesus to be the Leader of your life, but you've possibly done everything wrong and evil by the world's standards in your past, you are still worthy to pray and be heard by the Creator of the universe.

---

[10] Isa 64:6

76

God is for you and not against you and is not waiting in heaven for you to do something bad so He can punish you, nor is He waiting to treat you extra special if you toss enough prayers up to Him.

So where does that leave us? Some would look at that and say, "Then why even pray or take time to ask God things when He is going to do anything He wants anyway?" Let me pause before I answer this. I cannot say I have all the answers about what prayer is and why we need to do it, but I have definitely had my paradigm challenged about what I have always known prayer to be. I had many nights of crying out to God and asking Him to heal me or, if nothing else, to please take the pain away. I remember many nights telling Him that I apologize for anything bad that I had ever done that may be causing my eye to rot out of my head.

Now that I am on the other side of those four and a half years of pain, I can say that I have a better understanding of what prayer is. It's an exercise in trust and in asking God for His will to be done in our lives. It is true that God will do what He thinks is best for us when we are following Him, but we can rest in the knowledge that He is only good and will always cause us to triumph no matter what circumstances present themselves in life. I really believe prayer is more about getting to know who God is than about what we can get from Him.

> I really believe prayer is more about getting to know who God is than about what we can get from Him.

That statement exposes a fundamental flaw in our society, which is "what can you do for me?" Look at our economy and the ethical problems with government officials or the self-indulgence we see in television or entertainment, for example. We have MP3 players (which I am listening to right now) that have the playlist WE want, and we don't have to consider anyone else's wishes. I say these things because it is not bad to want certain things for yourself, but the problem comes when you have no regard for the people around you and become consumed with self-indulgence.

When we understand that we are communicating with God to get to know Him better, we will not question why He does what He does–and no matter what happens in life, we will approach it with wholehearted trust in God to bring us through. This is not blindly (no pun intended) accepting pain and negative things, because it's true that the devil will try to afflict us, but we will come to God in child-like faith, asking Him to change things in our life. We will be praying from a perspective that is asking God to help show us the big picture. If this concept can be grasped before the pain hits in life, I believe we will do much better with learning the "what do You want me to learn?" when we go through pain instead of worrying about the "why is this happening to me?"

The second pitfall that can happen with pain is spiritual arrogance. This is an interesting beast and can consume a person without that person even realizing it's happening. Of all the things I have learned while being sick, this is the one that I believe is the hardest to control or just fix. I believe there can be an unspoken fraternity of people who have gone through pain. You join it by going through something so terrible that, to explain it or to remember what happened to you, there is a wilting inside of you that is unexplainable.

The arrogance comes from thinking that what you went through and what God taught you qualifies you–and you alone–to be able to talk with a select group of people about pain. You feel that, to everyone else who has never dealt with your type of pain, you can say, "You just can't understand what I went through or what I am dealing with." You have installed a red phone to Jesus in your life that only you can use. It's as if Jesus only talks to *you* on a regular basis to solve the ills of the world through your immense and all-encompassing knowledge of dealing with pain. For you, the motivation in life is not to let people know that you are praying for them or that you have an ability to know how to lift their situation in prayer. It is to let all around you know that you have a scar from life's hurts that qualifies you as a part of the Pain Fraternity.

The way to deal with this is to keep a perspective on our pain and understand that everyone in life will go through something that he or she considers painful. One other thing that can signify you are in danger of this arrogance is when you hear of the pain someone else is going through, and you compare it to what you have been through. There have been times when I have heard of someone who is going through something, and I have said to myself, "Yeah, but they aren't worried about going blind or dying from some disease in their body that the doctors don't understand."

The best thing to help me deal with this is to remember the stories I heard when I sat in the sick room at the Arthritis Clinic, receiving my Remicade treatments. I would talk to people and hear that some of them were younger than I was and had some incurable disease that Remicade could only suppress and not cure. It helped me to have perspective and to realize I didn't have it so bad in the grand scheme of things. I am on the other side of being sick, and I believe that God has used a process of things to help heal me. It was not an overnight healing of my body and the calming of my immune system. It was a journey of learning to trust in God and learning to lean on the friends and family God had placed around me.

The third and longest-lasting pitfall is being stuck on what God did for me in my past and not what He has done today. When this first came to my mind, I immediately dismissed it as an attack of the devil, that the devil wanted me to

> It was not an overnight healing of my body and the calming of my immune system. It was a journey of learning to trust in God and learning to lean on the friends and family God had placed around me.

develop resentment toward God for allowing that pain in my life to be my teacher of sorts. This has been a huge obstacle for me since I have been feeling better after having been so sick; I get stuck in the past of what Jesus did for me. The people in this world are looking for answers personally, professionally, and spiritually. I know that, because of the physical pain that happened to me, I now have a platform to speak into their lives, because many people have pain and don't know how to deal with it.

If God is not doing something fresh or new in my life today, then there is a problem. The pain I went through makes for a nice interesting story, but it goes no further if I am not growing spiritually beyond it. Hopefully, it is nothing as dramatic as facing losing my eye again, but I know that our life experiences are what make us who we are and that knowledge we gain from those experiences needs to be shared with the world.

Holy Crap Moment:

Stop now. Take an inventory of what fresh and new things God is doing in your life. If you can't think of any, maybe it is time for a change of perspective in which you begin to look at life expecting the positive instead of expecting the negative. Write down and keep in a prominent place one new thing you know God is doing in your life or that you would like Him to do in your life. Thank God each morning for His fresh new work in you.

Take a Moment

_____

_____

_____

_____

We can get stuck re-living our negative experiences if we continue to stare at the scars of pain in our lives. We need to see them and let them be used for God's glory, but if we are not growing as a person and experiencing God, new and fresh, every day of our lives to deepen our relationship with Jesus, then we are only living from event to event in our lives. Instead, we need to be developing a victorious life that makes people who don't know Jesus want to know Him.

Most people know very well how to live from problem to problem. A truly fruitful and vibrant relationship with Jesus is not supposed to be living from problem to problem but from glory to glory. I once heard a great preacher, Joseph Garlington, say, "We need to be living from the 'up's' in life and not the 'down's'." The *"to"* of "from glory to glory" can be described as all the crap that happens in life that we may not understand or that feels painful to us, emotionally or physically. These are really meant to perfect our character and help us have a greater understanding of who we are inside. I believe that is the change that happens when you ask Jesus into your heart and is the key paradigm shift that Jesus has to offer people. God wants us not merely surviving life's pains but living from God's glory moments in our lives. Instead of just living to avoid pain, we begin to live life from a sense of purpose and a realization that we are part of something much greater than we could ever be on our own.

I understood this even when I was going through the pain of my eye. I had people around me who wanted to see me win and to come through an amazingly terrible and trying time that would shape who I am today. I am writing this book not to tritely tell you to speak five promises from God and everything will be made better. I'm writing it to tell you that I was not able to pray, but I trusted the loving and powerful group of people around me (my parents, sister, wife, and church family) who prayed prayers for me that I could never pray on my own during that time.

This was that time when I was on *spiritual* life-support. I needed all the things they were praying for me, but I had no strength to pray them for myself. It was for a season and was necessary, but I needed to learn how to "breathe" on my own and start to pray the prayers of faith and trust in God's power and wisdom which I had known as a child. My family and friends, who prayed life-support prayers for me, are the ones who helped me through the "to" parts of my life as I went from "glory to glory" these past few years. I am forever grateful to them and for the prayers they prayed for me. Because God does hear prayer and because they never quit praying, I am now in a position to share my perspective on pain and the changes that have happened inside of me. It is positively affecting the people around me who need to not only hear my story but also watch me and see how I am going to grow from the things that happened to me and my wife.

The final pitfall that can happen with pain is directly linked to the last point. Going through pain does not just make us stronger; it also shows how strong or weak we really are in ourselves. This is not a pitfall if pain shows the strength of your relationship with God, but I was a by-product, rather, of it showing me how weak my relationship with God was. What a huge eye-opener that was in finding out just how much I *didn't* know God!

Pain is what I call the great *exposer*. I can vividly remember sitting on the couch in my house after the MRI test (which thankfully came back negative). I had never felt so far away and abandoned by God as I did waiting for the results at that moment. This Assemblies of God preacher, this kid who had always done everything right by the Church's standards, came to the realization that he didn't know God as well as he thought he did. I found myself feeling like all of the teens I had ever counseled about how important it is to know God and have a personal relationship with Him. Before I got sick, I thought I had a pretty good relationship with Jesus. I had all the right answers and the right points to give people to make *their* lives better, but now I was faced with the fact that I felt a stranger to God myself. Everything I had ever grown to know and had studied all my life to become was not enough to get me out of my situation.

The reaction to pain in a person's life will tell more about a person and where he or she is in life than any words spoken from his mouth. It is the perfect example of actions speaking louder than words. I would have never known these things about myself if I hadn't have gone through this episode of pain. I know the things I knew *about* God were not a lie, but I didn't have a revelation of who God was in *my* life to compliment the knowledge I had *about* God. You get this revelation by spending what I call *non-required* time with Him. This is not being *compelled* to spend time because of the result of a bad doctor's diagnosis or because of losing all your money in the stock market or finding out something so terrible that needs a request to the "Big Guy in the Sky." It is just a desire to spend time with God because you want to know His heart and His plan for your life. There's really no other way to get it.

Holy Crap Moment

If you have a relationship with Jesus, then do an evaluation of how well you know Him. Do you just have all the right answers for people, or do you have a working and fulfilled relationship with Jesus that is willing to be tested and improved even if it's painful? I am asking if you trust Jesus enough in your relationship that you don't need to ask Him why you are going through something and you instead tell Him, "Okay, let the lesson begin." If you don't know Jesus, what do you do to deal with pain in your life? We are all guaranteed to have pain in our lives, no matter who we are, but we all have an option to just survive it or to learn from it.

A relationship with Jesus gives you the ability to live above pain in your life and become a better person, not only for yourself but for others.

Take a Moment

_____

_____

_____

_____

The most important thing I have learned about pitfalls is to understand that just getting through pain in your life is not good enough. You will also deal with other issues related to that pain in your life. The things I have shared are only a handful of the revelations I have received, and I am sure there are more things God wants to show me and teach me to help me become an even greater reflection of Him. We are all in danger of thinking we have everything figured out when we stop realizing there will always be one more thing to learn.

Even though I didn't see it at the time, God was preparing me for this time in my life. I had to realize that trusting in Him was more important than getting my way. I also realized that the pain I experience in life needs to be not a measure of my spirituality but rather a motivation to care for a world that doesn't know His love, but still needs it. I believe we were created for God and His will. That may be hard for some people to hear, but I would rather trust the One whom I believe built the universe and everything in it than one who has built a car, a website, or something

> . . . I would rather trust the One whom I believe built the universe and everything in it than one who has built a car, a website, or something else on this earth.

else on this earth. Ephesians 1:4-6 talks about how God chose us before the creation of the world. I was amazed at the number of times this passage mentioned "He." For **He** chose us in **Him** [Christ] before the creation of the world to be holy and blameless in **His** sight. In love **He** predestined us to be adopted as **His** sons through Jesus Christ, in accordance with **His** pleasure and will– to the praise of **His** glorious grace, which **He** has freely given us in the One **He** loves[11]

I know the pain I went through not only made me a better person but also caused my heart to be closer to God and gave me a better understanding of His plan for my life. I believe my circumstances convinced me even more that I have more growing to do, and I am determined to change this world with the power of this Jesus operating at full capacity in my life. Even that statement sounded like cheesy, religious jargon to me before I got sick. Now,

---

[11] NIV Translation

there is no other option for me, and I'm thankful that an eye condition helped this stubborn church kid understand he needs God and the power of the family of God in order to be everything God has called him to be.

Chapter 8
Accept the Challenge

There are two very specific and distinct types of change in a person's life. They are changes that you control and determine and the changes of life that we have no control over. The former is related to the decisions we make in life or the changes we make that we feel are necessary to become a better person. This can be anything from eating better and exercising more to reading more, talking to Jesus more, or really anything that we do that makes us a better person. We make these changes not because we feel we are obligated to by someone or something else but because we know it's the best thing for us. The other kind of change that we deal with in life is change that we cannot control. These include physical illness in a person or in a family member, mental struggles or challenges that come from the crap of life, or generally anything we consider painful in life and that is a divergence from everyday life.

Holy Crap Moment

When we are going into a season that we know is going to be difficult, our minds will naturally play out all the worst-case scenarios for the situation, especially if you are a worrier like I was. Maybe you are going through a difficult situation right now in life. Take a Moment and step back mentally from the firestorm. Understand that there are things you can control, such as your emotional response to situations, and things you cannot control, such as circumstances in life. When you see your situation in this way, it can help to keep a healthy "non-freaked out" perspective on things. Take a Moment and write out the things you CAN control in your situation and the things you CANNOT control.

Take a Moment

_____

_____

_____

_____

We are all guaranteed pain of all kinds in life. The difference is how we deal with those changes of life. It was hard for me to deal with the crap or change in my physical body because I felt I didn't deserve what was happening to me. I sat and listened to the ophthalmologist tell me that my eye was being eaten away, and I just couldn't believe it. The ironic thing is that I had preached these same words about being prepared for the pains of life and having a good attitude in it all through my pastoral career, and yet when it happened to me, I was so mad at God. I guess I knew that pain was a fact of life–for everyone else.

This attitude that was unearthed in me was a direct indicator of how little I had practiced what I preached. In all those messages, I had spoken of the importance of making personal change in a person's life. Yet it was something I had not done myself, unfortunately. Follow me here: if we are not changing the things about us that we CAN control, and then we have the guaranteed changes of life affect us that we CANNOT control, we are going to be in trouble and will probably not be able to deal with the crap that comes with living life.

Within about three minutes of the eye doctor explaining my eye situation to me, I had a super-charged revelation of the condition of my walk with God: shallow but very strong on the surface. This meant I had all the right answers for everyone else and none for myself. I was the biggest, crying, complaining person I knew for about four and a half years. The change I could control could not keep up with the change I could NOT control. I didn't trust that God had my best interests in mind, nor did I trust that He was hearing the desperation in my voice when I complained to Him that I was in pain.

This chapter is about taking inventory of the things in your life you need to change, not because I make you feel bad or tell you Jesus would be disappointed in you if you don't change. Rather, it's to help you maybe be pre-emptive in dealing with the pains and crap or changes of life. Sadly, most positive change we make in our lives comes from a negative change experience. We don't start eating healthy until we are scared into it by a nasty doctor's report or maybe by experiencing a heart attack of some sort. We don't start exercising until we start to feel crappy, emotionally or physically, about ourselves. We don't start going to church and talking to Jesus again until we are faced with something we can't reason away or is so painful that we think no one in this world would understand the depth of our pain. We don't start saving money until we can't pay our bills, and we get so overwhelmed with credit that we give up. We are generally creatures of comfort, and we take the path of least resistance. The problem with that kind of thinking is, if you are not voluntarily changing things about yourself to make yourself better, you are allowing the changes of life to dictate who you are and how you act. I will not let the change I CANNOT control decide for me the changes I CAN control.

Let me challenge you in a couple of areas in your life concerning change you can control.

1st Change Challenge: Be involved in church

I serve Jesus, and I make the decisions I do in my life not because I think I'm better than anyone else or that God will be mad at me if I don't serve Him but because I believe that is the best thing for my life. I know many people who are still trying to find happiness in all kinds of things, including anger at the church. That sounds like an opposing statement–to find happiness in anger. But I have seen it more than one time in a person's life. I have said this once, and I will say it many more times: in many ways, the church body and the family of believers is the reason why I got through my physical challenges these past few years. I know that God placed those people in my life to encourage me, strengthen me, kick my butt when I needed it, and generally help me be the best I could be when I was faced with the worst time of my life.

The change I am talking about here is a change of how we view the Church. The Church has gotten a pretty bad rap the past few years, and I believe it has turned many people off from being involved and from really integrating themselves into a body of believers. I know that I am a huge people person and love to have people around me all the time, but this is greater than personality or even personal preference. This is about the power of personal contact. This is about the strength you receive when you put yourself in a place to reach out to people, and they reach out to you. You may say, "Brian, I am not like you. I'm not a 'people-person' and I like to keep to myself." The blunt truth is that reaching out to people and positioning yourself to let them reach out to you is *good* for you and will bring healthy change in your life.

Holy Crap Moment

We were created to need human interaction, and this may be a time to evaluate why you feel like you like to keep to yourself. I am only saying this because we are products of our upbringing and pasts, and I want you to experience–or at least start–a journey of healing if there is something deeper that needs to be worked through in your life. I am not trying to force a point with you– just offering you a chance to get healing if it is needed.

Take a Moment

_____

_____

_____

_____

As I have mentioned earlier in this book, I know that the Church has its problems and is not perfect by any means. But think of my perspective: not only did I have the benefit of a godly, Bible-believing church family, which included my wife, but I also had one of the founding pastors of our church, World Evangelist Marilyn Hickey, call me every day for about five months in the worst and crappiest part of my sickness. Not only did Pastor Marilyn give me life-saving, personal support and care, but a man on staff at my church, Jim, along with his wife, JoAnn, prayed with me every single time I saw them at church or at work. My cousins Stephen and DeDee committed to pray every day for me and were also an integral part of my emotional and spiritual support network. As if they were not enough, I would have to mention all the people who stopped me in the halls at church or took me to lunch or coffee when I was no longer even on staff for those eleven months. I wouldn't be here today to share my story and to encourage you to keep going if it were not for these people. I literally saw the goodness and greatness of God through His people in the church when I was in my darkest hour.

Holy Crap Moment:

Maybe as you read this book, you realize it is your time to change and get involved in a good Jesus-focused and Bible-based church so that you can be around people who want to see you succeed in life. Don't let an eye condition or some other type of terrible crap force you to consider why you are not involved in a church body. A few distinct qualities of the kind of church or home group that I refer to above is that it **reveals**, **challenges**, *and* **encourages**. *It reveals items in your life that need work and are standing in the way of you becoming the person God has always meant for you be, it challenges your mind AND heart to evaluate your effectiveness in all areas of your life, and it encourages you to keep going and not give up on life in hard situations.*

Take a Moment

_____

_____

_____

_____

2nd Change Challenge: Have an attitude of gratefulness

Think about this statement: gratefulness provides an atmosphere for change. This was another one of those principles which I didn't understand until about four years into my sickness. If you haven't noticed, I am trying to set you up for greatness. I want you to be able to read the pages of this book and learn from my mistakes. I am not saying I did everything wrong in the past few years, but I did enough things wrong to the point at which I might be able to help you be further along than I was in my pain. In the book of Luke in the Bible, there is a great example of thankfulness about ten lepers (outcasts with a terrible skin disease):

> While Jesus was on his way to Jerusalem, He was going through the area between Samaria and Galilee. As He came into a small town, ten men who had a skin disease met Him there. They did not come close to Jesus but called to Him, "Jesus! Master! Have mercy on us!"
>
> When Jesus saw the men, He said, "Go and show yourselves to the priests."
> As the ten men were going, they were healed. When one of them saw that he was healed, he went back to Jesus, praising God in a loud voice. Then He bowed down at Jesus' feet and thanked Him. (And this man was a Samaritan.) Jesus said, "Weren't ten men healed? Where are the other nine? Is this Samaritan the only one who came back to thank God?" Then

Jesus said to him, "Stand up and go on your way.
You were healed because you believed."[12]

Did you read those verses correctly? There were ten lepers who had an incredibly terrible skin disease and were outcasts to society. It says that nine went on their merry way, yet only *one* came back to actually thank Jesus for what He did! This portion of scripture always astounds me with the contrast of gratefulness and ungratefulness, all in the same section of scripture. The one made the effort to go back to where Jesus was to thank Him, but the others so quickly forgot that not only were they healed but also that an amazing lifestyle change had just been given to them. I believe gratefulness is a key element in making it through a rough time in your life. It takes the sting out of a painful situation by focusing on what you do have instead of being concerned with what you don't have.

I remember when Pastor Marilyn told me that I needed to keep a journal of positive things in my life when I was really sick. One entry from June 5, 2005, read that the most positive thing I could think of that day was the United States being ahead in the medal

> I believe gratefulness is a key element in making it through a rough time in your life. It takes the sting out of a painful situation by focusing on what you do have instead of being concerned with what you don't have.

---

[12] Luke 17:11-19 (NCV)

count at the Olympics. I looked at it just the other day and remembered where I was at that moment in my life–so pitiful. I had a sudden flood of emotions and remembered how I felt that day when I wrote those simple, and goofy to me, words on that paper. I can remember not even being able to see the paper very well when I wrote that because of the central cirrus happening in my good eye from taking the prednisone steroid to help my bad eye. Central cirrus is a bubble of fluid that collects in an eye (my good eye, of course) and bends any straight line in your vision. I know now that being grateful in painful situations helps us realize the things we do have as we face what we are losing.

Holy Crap Moment:

Do you have something going wrong in your life that you need to find something positive about? Go ahead right now and think of one positive thing that is happening in your life, juxtaposed with the one (or maybe more) negative thing(s) happening. You might even want to record them in your own journal, as was recommended to me, to help you keep looking for the positives. And remember, you can also go to HolyCrapBook.com for occasional blog posts to encourage you if you are in a difficult place in life right now.

Take a Moment

_____

_____

_____

_____

One other huge thing I realized was that I needed to be grateful for my wife, Yolanda. There were times when I was not very nice to her–or to my dog, Wilson, for that matter. I was only concerned with what was going on physically in my body, and I was ignoring the fact that Yolanda was there with me through everything. I can say that in *countless* ways she was there. In the darkest hour, she would not let me speak negative things over my life. She was strong beyond her years. I remember many times when I would be lying on the couch in front of the TV. Yolanda would ask me, "Who are you?" And I would say, "Just a guy waiting to go blind and probably die early." The answer she was looking for was, "I am an overcomer and will not let disease rule my life. I am a child of Christ, and He still has me in His hand."

We were just talking about those moments the other day, and I could remember them as if they were yesterday. I know those things that I was saying were from the thoughts of suicide and hopelessness in which I existed. I had allowed myself to become a victim and to believe the lies from the devil in my head. I know that people deal with depression and dark thoughts of despair. Even as I type this sentence I am praying for you to be free from those thoughts, whether they are from something chemical that needs to be healed or just demonic harassment to keep you from knowing the authority you have when you call Jesus the Lord of your life. I am forever grateful to Yolanda and for the strength that she had in our marriage when I was not able to be the man I needed to be in our home. I look back now at the personal change I needed to make by being grateful for things when I was sick, but at the time, I was not a very grateful person. I was better at complaining about my situation than realizing what God had given me in the middle of an all-consuming and terrible storm.

If you don't feel like you have that person in your life to help lift you up and to keep you going and not give up, I am praying for you and believing that God will bring comfort and a sense of hope when there seems to be no hope. The Bible has a great portion of scripture that talks about finding the peace of God that exceeds anything we can understand and that it actually guards our hearts and our minds in God, through Jesus Christ. [13]There was a time that I didn't want to pay attention to that scripture, but if I had, it would have given me something that I really needed at the time–the peace of God. I am praying also right now for you to have that kind of peace that seems crazy to others. Just hang on one more day. If this book can get you through one more day, I have done my job in being obedient to write these words on paper.

Holy Crap Moment:

Please evaluate your gratitude level now before the changes of life come that you cannot control. Maintaining gratitude will keep your head above water and your mind above the storm. It will turn every pain into a time of realization about what you have rather than what you don't.

Take a Moment

_____

_____

_____

_____

[13] Php 4:7 (NLT)

3rd Change Challenge: Decide to be happy because happiness is a decision, not a condition.

I really think that happiness is different than gratefulness. Even when I learned how to be grateful, I still was not happy. Think about it this way: gratefulness is for you inside, but happiness is for others. The reason I could be grateful but not happy was that I was still dealing with selfishness when I was sick. I think a HUGE component of sickness is selfishness. I was coming to grips inside with the physical condition of my life and how to be grateful in the midst of the experiences I was going through (even though they may have seemed terrible), but I was allowing the presence of sickness to dictate to me how I would act. How many times do we allow circumstances to control how we feel or react to life? I don't think you need to have an eyeball rotting out of your head to understand the power that emotions can have in painful circumstances to lead us to poor decisions.

I used to think that how I felt was a direct result of my level of happiness. I now believe this is a myth and can cause a person to be moody and unstable in his or her emotional state from day to day. Even though the person has an understanding that his life circumstances have a purpose or meaning for him, he can still be an unhappy person. No one likes to be around a moody person; people love to be around others who speak positively about situations and who decide to be happy in the face of difficult circumstances.

Holy Crap Moment:

Decide today that you are not going to let circumstances in your life affect who you are or dictate your level of happiness. Write down one thing in your life you are dealing with that has the potential to keep you unhappy and what you are going to do, intentionally, to be happy in midst of that storm.

Take a Moment

_____

_____

_____

_____

I really know now that, when people see you having a positive attitude in the middle of your crap, it's more effective in bringing them hope and encouragement in their crap than having the right words to speak to them. I am not saying that everything we do needs to be about other people, but we are beings who need each other to exist and to live a fulfilled life. Many people use isolation as a tool to stay happy or to achieve a version of happiness that they can feel comfortable in without having to confront the issues that cause pain in life. Covering up pain and faking happiness is not what I am talking about here. I am only saying that we need to find the balance of gratefulness–for our benefit and happiness–for the benefit of others, both of which cause us to be productive members of society.

It took me almost five years of ridiculous medical bills, pain beyond explanation, and discovering that I was very shallow in my relationship with my God to learn this simple truth: change your life before the changes of life dictate who you become.

Holy Crap Moment:

Change for you may be calling out to God. This may sound ethereal and not specific enough, but it really is just calling out to Jesus and telling Him that you want Him to take control of your life and to help you not let your circumstances determine your level of happiness. Maybe there is a church around you that preaches the Bible and has those three qualities I spoke of earlier; it reveals things that have hindered you, it challenges you to change, and it encourages you to keep going, even when it seems difficult. You need to go this Sunday and do something different than what you have been doing in order to get different results. I believe that those who seek the Lord will find Him! It's time to start, or maybe restart, the search.

Take a Moment

_____

_____

_____

_____

Chapter 9
Dealing with Pain

One amazing thing about the way God created us is that we all have coping mechanisms we use in reaction to pain of any kind. Maybe we put up extra walls or barriers to protect ourselves mentally. Maybe we eat until we forget our circumstances, or we don't eat because we are so sad and confused about life. I experienced the gamut of emotional coping mechanisms when I was sick: distancing myself from life and people whom I knew loved me, not eating correctly for months, sleeping all day so that I didn't think about the pain I was in or the horrible future I had convinced myself was mine, worrying to a point that I considered killing myself. I firmly believe that God has given me principles to help deal with pain in my life, and I want to share them with you so maybe they can help you through the painful situation you are dealing with right now or that you know you still need to deal with.

I want to say something before I get into dealing with pain in life. Please remember that no matter how you feel physically, mentally, or spiritually, anger and hate for someone or for God will NEVER improve the quality of your life and will actually degrade it. Think about this verse from the Bible: "...for man's anger does not bring about the righteous life that God desires."[14]

I love this verse because it says that the fact that you getting mad about something won't resolve anything and is not a part of

---

[14] James 1:20 (NIV)

the life that God wants you to have. The verse before talks about being quick to listen and slow to speak, two things in this life that are probably not first on the list of reactions we are hurt or offended in some way.

Holy Crap Moment:

If you have never read the Bible, it is such a cool book. I want to encourage you to check it out. Even if you read a proverb a day, it can really be a great step to putting the Word of God into your life, and you will see how you'll change in wonderful ways. You can either view it as a book of rules or as a guidebook for life to help you make great decisions.

Take a Moment

_____

_____

_____

_____

One of the intentions of this book is to help you re-evaluate your life and actions if you have been offended by a stranger, a family member, a friend, or even God. Pain can come in all forms and can take us from a place where we are solidly in a healthy, personal relationship with God to a place we don't even like to be in at times. One thing is for sure: if you are alive, there are enough offenses that happen for a lifetime in our world. The evidence of an unhealed offense in your life could be that you say stupid, reactive things or act in ways that can be hurtful to yourself or others. Our behaviors sometimes are barometers of internal pain.

I can remember some amazing summer camps while growing up in Montana. Something the late Keith Elder, the District Youth Director of Montana at the time, would say about kids causing trouble at camp really stuck with me. It was that kids don't cause problems; they reveal the problems they are dealing with in their lives. I think people *revealing* problems and not necessarily *causing* them applies not only to kids but also to adults. Our actions in life are normally a reaction to the physical or emotional scars from our past or to a wound we are currently dealing with in some way or another.

I contend that current pain from past hurts in life is a result of surviving painful situations and not truly learning from them. I think this can produce a huge misconception in someone dealing with hurt in life: just because you go through something painful in life does not mean that you have really learned anything. We can confuse *surviving* with *learning* very easily, and it is something we need to consider when we go through episodes of pain. The Bible has an interesting take on painful situations in life: "More than that, we rejoice in our sufferings, knowing that suffering produces endurance, and endurance produces character, and character produces hope..."[15]

It is hard to believe, but we can actually GROW from a painful situation. It says that we can rejoice in suffering knowing that we are building endurance for life. I do not believe that God causes painful situations in our life to teach us lessons. There are many other ways He uses, including direction in the Bible, to help get the best out of us. At the same time, we are not promised that life will

---

[15] Rom 5:3-4 (NIV)

be void of pain. Those painful situations provide opportunities to build endurance that CAN produce character, which leads to hope. Just going through crap in life does not guarantee we will have "good fruit" in life because we only survived.

This is where our focus and our doing a couple of very important things put us in a place to win and see victory. One is to realize that the devil hates us and wants us to fail in life–fail miserably. God, on the other hand, has great plans to prosper us and to give us a bright hope and a future. At the same time, we are not God, and we don't understand why things happen the way they do in life. The only thing we can control in painful life situations is our attitude and our willingness to allow trouble to bring out the best in us. Below are some pain principles that can aid in that and can possibly help you move from *surviving* to *learning* in the crap of life.

The first pain principle is to realize that people who ask how you are genuinely care. If we do not purpose to believe the very best about people, we will have a very pessimistic view of life and will probably not be any fun to be around. I have never been so short with so many people in my whole life as when I was sick. I am the type of person who would prefer to have people around me twenty-four hours a day, seven days a week. I feel it is my God-given duty to bring fun to the party and make sure I am the center of it. (Maybe I shouldn't have said that second part.) When I got sick, I didn't want to be around anyone, talk to anyone, be prayed for by anyone, or really have any human contact.

Being a pastor presents an interesting dynamic when you're sick. To be a good pastor, you really need to love people, and it kind of defeats the purpose of being a pastor if you don't like being around people. After I was sick and had to step out of my youth pastor role, I would actually try to find alternate ways out of the sanctuary if I saw that people from the church on a Sunday morning were going to come up and talk to me. I just didn't want to talk to people about my eye. I didn't want them staring at me because my eye was red and inflamed or because the muscles in my face were reacting to the pain by twitching and kind of hanging on my left side. It was very hard for me to not think that people were just trying to annoy me with questions about my health. This is related to the selfishness of pain I talked about earlier.

Think about it this way: I believe that my sickness was an activator to help improve other people's prayer lives. I may have run from people who wanted to know how I was doing, but I may also have actually robbed them of an opportunity to grow in their walk with God. I have an awesome family, and I can remember getting a card in the mail from my Aunt Barb and her prayer team at their church in Washington State. It was a card of encouragement, signed by my aunt and about eight other people whom I had never met before. That card really blew me away, and I had an epiphany at that moment about my pain: what I was going through was not just about me, and there were people who were praying for me that I had never even met!

Now I am not saying that every person who wants to know how you are doing has pure intentions. Some people are just busybodies and want to have the inside skinny on your life so they can know something that others may not know. I have grown up in the church all my life and know that these people will always be around, but there are also others who genuinely care about how you are doing and maybe just say it or show it in a way that comes across to you as not caring or flippant of your situation. All I am saying is that we need to be careful not to cut people off or run from those who genuinely care about us.

I also had people in my life who didn't know Jesus, and they were watching me to see how I would react to them; they were just kind of checking up on me to see just how I was dealing with the pain. I am a firm believer that anyone who does not have a functional relationship with Jesus is searching for peace in his or her own way, and that includes figuring out how to deal with pain. I realize I had an advantage over others who go through pain and don't have Jesus. Even though I went through a time of questioning whether God had my best interests in mind, I always knew He was with me. Even when I was acting like a child in many ways, He was waiting there for me to quiet down, and then just at the right moment, He would send someone into my life to minister to me even when I didn't want to hear it.

Holy Crap Moment:

Is there someone you know that you need to talk to and see how they are doing? Just take a couple of minutes now and say a prayer for them and ask God to intervene in their life. You don't have to have a special gift to be able to pray. It really is just as simple as opening your mouth, addressing God (aka, saying "Hi"), and telling Him what is on your mind and heart. That's really all He is looking for!

Take a Moment

_____

_____

_____

_____

Even though I see people's authentic concern now as an important principle, I know there were many more times I could have been encouraged and lifted up if I had understood this principle earlier in my pain. Essentially, we need the genuine love of people to carry us sometimes, and we need to be willing to be put on spiritual life-support during those times for our spiritual self to reset so that we can spiritually function normally again.

The second pain principle is that pain can be a wonderful reminder of how to encourage others and pray for their circumstances. I talked earlier about how pain can be a way for you to improve the quality of your life by changing your perspective on it. This point is more that, by your going through pain, you are now equipped to help encourage others through their pain and what is happening to them. If you are a Christian, going through or having gone through pain motivates you to pray for people when you hear about crap they are going through.

Holy Crap Moment:

If you are a follower of Christ and a part of a church body, you have a RESPONSIBILITY to care about others in your church. One of the GREATEST and WORST things I hear from people who have been burned by churches is the way that Christians treat each other. There is an attractive power that is generated in the church for a person who doesn't have a relationship with Jesus when followers of Christ treat each other with godly respect and concern.

Take a Moment

_____

_____

_____

_____

God designed the church body to lift one another up and be there for one another. I started something amazing with my Facebook account that I know came completely from God. One day per week, I update my status by asking for prayer requests that I will lift up during that day. It is amazing, the number of people who respond to me and ask me to pray for them. I also encourage them to post testimonies about what God has done through prayer to help encourage those who are still waiting for their answer.

I do not consider myself to be someone who knows everything about terminal disease or being sick for many years. I actually feel blessed that I could have a few years of pain to experience the things I did so I can better relate to people of all walks of life who have some sort of crap going on in their lives. I was sick just long enough to have the "we don't know what else we can do" conversations with the doctor, have a major test done on my body, and be sent home to wait for the results, hoping it wasn't cancer. I was sick just long enough to have the privilege of spending some time at the Arthritis Clinic in the Remicade room and hearing so many heart-breaking stories.

I consider my experiences to have been wonderful opportunities to have a peek into the lives of people who were dealing with life-altering disease and to encourage me in a new way to pray for them and believe for God's best for them. I have allowed the pain I went through be a catalyst of sorts to help me understand how to pray and have a heart that goes out to every person who has a serious need in their lives. If you don't know Jesus as your best friend, then you really need to have that connection in your life to get a full grasp of what I am saying. This is more than just having good and positive thoughts about a person. It is doing something in the spiritual realm to lift a person's needs before a God who will always be there to listen, care, and help you use your difficult circumstances for a greater good than just getting through the inevitable pain in life.

Holy Crap Moment:

*Being a "strong" person and just keeping good and positive thoughts going will not make real change in your life and probably won't be enough to bring you through really tough times. When you have a relationship with Jesus though, you change from just trying to survive by your positive mental outlook alone to now having a deeply personal connection to God. And it's **His** love for you and **His** power at work in you which makes real and lasting change.*

Take a Moment

_____

_____

_____

_____

The third principle of pain is that we can never forget that our attention or focus in a storm is much more important than our actions. Sometimes we think there is something we can DO to change the fact that we have pain in our lives–that if we take *action*, we can stop the pain. We all have certain innate reactions to painful situations, and sometimes, I think we really believe that if we DO something different, our situation will change. I am not talking about boneheaded things we do that bring pain or crap on ourselves, such as letting our mouths react to a situation before our brains have time to process what's coming out or putting ourselves in some kind of danger because we are looking to be more funny than responsible. Those kinds of storms can definitely be averted or changed by making better choices in life.

I am talking about painful situations that come up in life that we have no control over. Actually, these are the kinds of things that happen to all of us and take us by surprise when we think that we are doing everything right and don't deserve what is happening. We reevaluate what we did to possibly have caused what is happening to us, but we just can't figure it out.

Intentional focus in a storm can be interpreted as the way you handle the situation. You realize that it's not what you do, but you have a great opportunity to learn a valuable life lesson to which others are probably not privy. Unfortunately, I was the "actions guy" through my pain. In the Bible, there was a guy named Peter whom the Bible says walked on water towards Jesus in the middle of a storm. But as soon as he took his eyes off of Jesus and fixed them on the stormy waves, he began to sink:

> "Lord, if it's You," Peter replied, "tell me to come to You on the water." "Come," He said. Then Peter got down out of the boat, walked on the water and came toward Jesus. But when he saw the wind, he was afraid and, beginning to sink, cried out, "Lord, save me!" Immediately Jesus reached out His hand and caught him. "You of little faith," He said, "why did you doubt?"

> And when they climbed into the boat, the wind died down. Then those who were in the boat worshiped Him, saying, "Truly you are the Son of God."[16]

He started thinking about his ACTIONS in the storm instead of his FOCUS, which said, "If that's Jesus, I need to get to Him even if I need to walk on water!" He started thinking about what *he* could do to get to Jesus instead of realizing that it was Jesus who was helping him walk on the water in the middle of the storm in the first place. When we understand that pain in life cannot be avoided by being a good person, by thinking positive thoughts, or by doing all the things to prevent pain in life, then we are taking steps toward becoming the type of person we need to be, not only for ourselves

---

[16] Matt 14:28-33 (NLT)

but also for the people around us who need to have hope in the middle of terrible and painful situations.

Life is, in some ways, a series of painful situations that we need to learn from as we get older and wiser in life. I mentioned this in an earlier chapter, but I feel it is so important that it bears repeating: we need to view pain in life as an opportunity to grow beyond the *why* is this happening to me, to *what* it is You are trying to teach me. We need to ask God to show us how to apply the things we learn in order to make us better people. If we will give people who ask us how we are doing the benefit of the doubt, use our times of pain to remember to pray for others, and never forget that our focus in a storm of life is more important than our actions, we position ourselves mentally for God to intervene in our situation, and we actually become the best version of ourselves for the benefit of others.

Chapter 10
Change You Control and
Change that Controls You

Pain changes lives. I mentioned in a previous chapter that pain can dictate how we spend our lives and the changes we have to endure. The pain that is guaranteed in life is a form of change that you cannot control. It is anything that happens to a person without reason or provocation and has the potential to alter the direction or career of a person or family if the pain is severe enough. This can be physical sickness in you or a family member, or it can be something emotional that stems from some traumatic event that happened to you or someone you know.

When my eye condition started, I was doing my best to be a positive influence on the world and help teens to see the importance of having God in their lives. I had a small vein in the lower part of my eye that became the center of massive and almost catastrophic damage to my eye from front to back. I still have most of my peripheral vision in that eye, but looking straight ahead, I have 20/400 vision. This was, and now still is, a change that occurred that I had to overcome. I have experienced a loss of depth perception in my vision that I have had to compensate for in order to drive, read, do computer work, ski, hike, and do other recreational activities. These changes were not things that happened to me because of something I did to myself; they were just the course of life that came with the sickness.

I don't plan to settle into this as a permanent outcome. I am expecting full restoration in my eye. Sometimes, there are changes that we have to adapt to in our lives. Sometimes they are permanent changes, and sometimes they are temporary. Some of them probably cannot be controlled by something we did or didn't do. This is my perspective on my healing and where I currently am with my eye. If I cannot believe that God wants to heal me, then there is a 100 percent chance that I will not be healed. But if I keep my eyes on Him and believe that I will see 100 percent again in both eyes, I provide an opportunity for God to do His part because I have done my part of lining up my faith with His grace. It is not about making God do anything that He is already willing and able to do. It is trusting that He has both my life on this earth and my eternity with Him all under control.

I grew up in church, and I was convinced that everything that happened to me was directly connected to my actions. If I read my Bible more, then good things would happen to me. If I prayed more and longer, then Jesus would certainly hear my request and do what I asked of Him because I was *putting in the time* to see things change. I thought I was impervious to bad things happening to me if I would do the things I needed to do in order to secure that guaranteed future. That one single flawed belief probably made my eye situation even harder to deal with because I didn't think I deserved what was happening to me. I don't really think that belief stemmed from the pastors I had in my life or from my parents; rather, it was just something that I grew to believe.

I had always been the good kid growing up, and good things had always happened to me. I had never experienced the type of change in life that dictates when you take medication, and that taking some of those medications could potentially have other harmful effects. I had never experienced painful change like having to step down from being a pastor for eleven months, having a limited income, and accruing thousands of dollars in medical bills and credit card debt. I really believed it was not yet time for me to deal with that kind of change in life. I believe there is a reason for everything we deal with in life, but we have the responsibility to do a few things ourselves.

Holy Crap Moment

If you are going through a change because of pain in your life, accept it as an opportunity to learn something you would never have been able to learn without it. If you have a family member going through that kind of pain change in life, then be the best support you can for them and purpose within yourself to encourage them with words and actions that will help them through the situation. If you have not been through the kind of pain that changes a person's life, then do everything you can now to prepare for dealing with those things and learning everything you can.

There is a full and powerful relationship with God that He offers everyone who believes in Him, but I never took full advantage of it when I was feeling good and had no real bad to deal with in life. This is a relationship that goes beyond the traditional forms of following Christ in going to church, reading your Bible, and praying. It is another level of connection to God that is focused on "how close can I get to God" and not "how far away can get from Him and still make it to heaven." All the things previously mentioned are important in the life of a person who claims to have a relationship with Jesus, but if it is purely focused on duty and not privilege, then people build a form of godliness without the power needed when times get tough. God has and knows everything you need, and it may be time for you to reach out to Him. You can go to HolyCrapBook.com right now and get resources to start your relationship with Jesus.

Take a Moment

_____

_____

_____

_____

That leads me to the second and more important half of this chapter. These are the changes of life that we CAN control. There are things that we can do to make the learning process easier in life and take us from being a survivor of painful situations to an ever-learning, ultra-productive member of society. The actions I mentioned earlier, praying and reading your Bible, are not negative things that fail to bring change in a person's life. But for me, it was the expectation I had that was bad, that if I did those good things in life no bad thing would happen to me.

You see, there is a power in life that comes from being proactive against unforeseeable change in your life. If you are going to the gym and working on ways to make yourself physically fit, then by that means you are changing something about yourself to possibly prevent sickness and live a longer life. If you choose on your own to go to church and be involved in people's lives on a spiritual level, while allowing them to be involved in your life, then you are being proactive in your mental and spiritual well-being.

The first kind of change I talked about can be seen when you don't take care of yourself, and you receive a negative doctor's report that makes a change in lifestyle dramatically and amazingly important. You can also be motivated to make a change in life when you go through something so traumatic that you feel empty and lost deep inside with a hole that only God can fill. And even if you didn't do the things to build any relationship with God, and now you feel compelled to go to church and get involved, your decision will get you on the right path.

Even if you didn't make the change proactively, God will rush in and fill that hole in your life. Bible reading is a wonderful way to learn about who God is and who He can be to you in your life. It is not a book of magic potions or a to-do list of life to be able to get something. It is the inspired Word of God, which we have on this earth to help us live the most fulfilled and successful life we can now and to have a hope and future of an eternity with Him. You don't get brownie points for reading it, and if you memorize it, it doesn't magically make you a better person. The Bible really is God's love letter and message to us of how much He's done for all of us, and it gives us a foundation, a strength, and a knowledge to use when times get bad. It gives us a firm foundation to be able to deal with the changes that come in life that we have no control over.

Prayer is also not a wish list to Jesus that we use to get what we want. It is communication with God in loving response to His love toward us. And that prayer communication teaches us more about who God is and what His plan is for our lives. It is a proactive activity we do to enhance our relationship with Jesus so that we are equipped when the painful changes of life come to affect who we are. All these things are changes that we can make for ourselves before the pains of life come.

Pain that happens in life is not going to MAKE who you are; it will show WHERE you are with yourself and with God. We have been misled into thinking that if we simply go through something painful in life, we are automatically going to be made a better person. When that change comes, we expect that we will be transformed into this amazing human being, able to grow from the ashes of hurtful circumstances into someone from whom the world will benefit. The fact is that when we go through a situation like that, we are met head-on with who we are and how we have prepared for that time in our life.

> Pain that happens in life is not going to MAKE who you are; it will show WHERE you are with yourself and with God.

I can say that I did not prepare very well for my eye situation and the things that were to follow for the next five years of my life. I had prepared myself, instead, to be a complainer, a skeptic of the Love of God, a whiner to my wife, and a questioner of everything I thought I believed in life. Unfortunately, I have extensive knowledge of these types of episodes, and it was painful to have to learn such an important life lesson.

I can remember moments in life when I was looking or waiting for the other shoe to drop when it came to my health. I turned into the kind of person who expected the bad and hoped for the best. I think that what I went through with all the medications I had to take and all the failures at finding a drug to fix my eye conditioned me, in a way, to expect defeat or a negative report. Looking back now, if my doctors actually had found something that would have regulated my immune system, I would still be on it today. I would not have been at that point of desperation; I would not have attended a National Day of Healing at my church and started the process of eliminating all medication from my life. Here is a perfect example of the actual "blessing" it was that the medical professionals I saw were only able to *diagnose* what I had and not the cause of it in order to *cure* my disease.

So, what is the point of this chapter? If you let crap happen to you before you decide to initiate change in your life, then you will always be shaped and molded by the circumstances around you. You will deceive yourself and say things such as, "I am not 'tied down to the dogma of religion' or the 'rules of church' or under the command and control of God," and you might think yourself privileged and free. No, you will be under the command and control of the painful situations of life and have no one and nothing to fall back on but your money, which is fleeting; your career, which can disintegrate in an instant; or your own mind, which can fail you.

Pain does not respect people, doesn't care how many worldly possessions you have, and can attack at any time with any amount of force, for any or no reason. God is actually the same way but with *opposite* qualifications: He doesn't show favoritism but loves you unconditionally; He loves you no matter what you do or don't own; and He will bless you at any time with any amount of force for any reason known only to Him. Intentional and unconditional love for you is His motivator!

As you can see, I am pretty passionate about this point because if you can get the concept of taking proactive measures against pain, then you can be a better person when the pain comes. I am not saying that the pain will not happen to you if you are proactive with change in your life. There are still people like my mother-in-law, who was a hero to me spiritually and who ate greens, exercised, and generally took care of her body, yet died of Lou Gehrig's disease or ALS during everything my wife and I were going through with my eye condition. The difference was that the changes my mother-in-law made in her life before she got sick prepared her for the situation in life that happened to her, and she went out of this world having touched people's lives with the love of Christ for a purpose greater than just her name being known as an evangelist.

I cannot say I am any closer to answering the question about why crappy things happen to good people. I had a revelation about my goodness when I got sick that helped me see that everything good I had ever done in my life was not enough to keep me out of the reach of pain. I do know now that because life is unpredictable, I need God more now than ever. I need to pray to know His heart and not pray to get what I want. I need to read my Bible because I want to know Him and know more about the things I can do to make this world a better place for everyone around me. I know I need to go to church because I was created to be in contact and communication with people who will have my back,

> I do know now that because life is unpredictable, I need God more now than ever.

spiritually and physically. I will need their support when I feel my world falling apart and their words to remind me about the incredible price that Jesus paid for my failures. I also want to be available to help my church family and give to them the motivation, the love, the listening ear, and the prayers that I received for five years of being sick and in despair.

Holy Crap Moment

I mentioned the Facebook Friend Prayer Day that I do on Tuesdays, so I want to challenge you to do the same! I have learned in today's society that there is nothing greater that I can do for someone than to love them like Jesus does and prove that statement by praying for them. It is fairly simple and only takes a few minutes to post on your wall. But please beware!! Praying for people, encouraging them, and seeing their lives change because you were simply praying for them can be addictive!

Take a Moment

_____

_____

_____

_____

I never want to be caught, as I was with my eye situation, discovering how little I know God or His character, and I never want to come so close to the point of wanting to end my life because I didn't see the value of it. Today can be the start for you of an amazing journey with God. It can be the start of an opportunity not to be reactive but rather to live a life that has a purpose and a meaning greater than just making money and living for self. I dare you to find out about the true nature of God and His plan for you. Don't just listen to what people have told you about God. Start a search for Him yourself in the Bible, and if you don't know where to start, you can go to HolyCrapBook.com for more information and start your journey today!

Chapter 11
Physical Sight Versus Spiritual Sight

"Get your eyes off your eye, and get your eyes on Me." This statement was something I believe God told me more than once while I was sick and living with complaints and negativity as my first reaction to everything. I was so focused on the physical damage in my eye that I was forgetting about my "spiritual sight," and I was allowing my health to direct my focus in life.

The level of deterioration in my eye was other-worldly to me. For instance, in the first few months of my eye situation, I was going to the doctor at least three times a week. Every visit to the ophthalmologist showed greater destruction in my eye than the previous visit, and I was now down to two hours of intermittent sleep a night because the pain never ceased. I can remember many times when Yolanda would try to encourage me in some way to keep my eyes on Jesus instead of my physical situation.

As I have previously said, I am naturally a very stubborn person who has to learn most things the hard way;, I don't let someone else help me by telling me how to change an attitude or general focus in my life before I will make the effort to change. Having no control over my health and no ability to change something in order to see a different result was very frustrating. What I didn't realize in those years was that I could ALWAYS choose to be in control of what I thought or felt in my situation; I just chose not to.

Holy Crap Moment:

Are you naturally a stubborn person? I can tell you from firsthand experience that stubbornness and painful situations do not mix well. Think about the reason why you are hard-headed in life. When we realize that other people's perspectives on how we do life can be very beneficial, we will be more flexible when the crap of life happens. Maybe take a few minutes and ask God to reveal an area of your life that needs correction.

Take a Moment

_____

_____

_____

_____

I knew God was encouraging me to do things or follow His lead inside the pain I was experiencing in my life. The problem was that I was strictly in stubborn survival mode and forgot that God could direct me and show me things while I was struggling. Unfortunately, I can only now look back on that process and feel a bit of regret for not choosing to listen to God and His leading in my life. This is really a different kind of feeling than I have ever experienced before. It's the kind of thing that moves me to the point of doing anything I can to caution you if you are in one of these two groups: you are either in the middle of pain in your life, and I want to help you to hang on for just one more day, or you are a person who has not yet gone through inevitable hurtful situations, and I want to help you change now to be prepared for it.

I honestly think it's vital for every person who calls Jesus his Friend and the Director of his life to be connected to a Bible-believing local church. I have listened to people these past years talk about how they are working on a relationship with Jesus that is independent of the local church. When I hear these things, I challenge those people to just get sick and see how important the family of God becomes. I know I have mentioned this earlier in the book, but what I went through really tested what I believed. I grew up in church, but when I got sick and couldn't pray the prayers that I was told would help me in my life, I had a first-hand revelation about the importance of the church body. I experienced the power of my personal family as well as my church family when they stepped up and helped me get through this time in my life.

I cannot look back and say that, if my relationship with Jesus had been better, I would have handled my situation differently. That would not be fair to what I believe God is doing in me now, as I now am able to have a very specific viewpoint about pain that I can share with the world. I agree that everyone is going to react to pain differently. I have talked to friends who told me their way of handling pain is that they are quoting favorite verses from the Bible in their struggle, or they are just trying to stay positive and not think about what is happening to them, whether it is physical or emotional. I have had one person in a painful situation tell me that I didn't know or understand what she and her family were going through, which I actually agreed with because, even if we go through the exact same pain, we can never really know what another person is battling with in her mind. I can only speak from my personal experience of dealing with pain. There is one constant with pain that I would like to address. To simplify it, I found that pain comes in three identifiable stages.

The first stage is the arrival of pain. You can know it's coming, so it's expected, or you can be unaware of its coming, so it's unexpected. It can come with or without provocation. The expected kind can be the emotional pain of an imminent divorce or maybe a terminally ill child that you are facing losing in the next few months. The unknown or unexpected can be the shock of being diagnosed with a rare form of cancer or having a family member get in an accident. For me, it was the possibility of losing my eye–and perhaps my life, if it turned out to be more than just an eye condition.

This stage of pain is the one that feels as if we still have control over the situation. Perhaps we strategize in our minds how we will deal with or walk through the pain that we see on the horizon or that may have just happened. We prepare ourselves, mentally and emotionally, for the worst case scenario. Or maybe we just ignore the fact that the pain is on its way, and we think that if we just don't identify what's coming, it won't really happen. If we are caught off-guard by this stage of pain, we go into survival mode, as I did, because we are just trying to keep our heads above the waters. Being a Christian did not preclude me from the arrival of pain, but it did give me an advantage in the way I was able to deal with that pain. That advantage was primarily because of the family of believers around me.

The second stage is the lifestyle of pain. This is the stage that feels like the pain will never end. This can last a few days, a few months, or a few years depending on the circumstances. For me, this was definitely when I felt the most helpless and most understood that my sickness was not under my control. I endured countless trips to the eye doctor to have my eye dilated and easily more than 200 trips to the rheumatologist to get my blood work done and get poked by a needle. It seems to me that in the past five years I have given gallons of blood. I am sure it hasn't been that much, but when you are in the lifestyle of pain, it can feel that way.

This stage is where depression can kick in from the relentless crashing of the waves of bad news and setback days. I had more than a few of those. This stage is where the needs of others disappear in the face of the needs of self, where selfishness is honed into a fine art form that we carry with us each day. This is the meat of the testing time that I believe really shows us just where we are with God in our lives. The problem is that if we don't know Jesus, –or we know Him but don't trust Him, this time is made exponentially worse.

I would complain about my life to my wife. She would ask me who I was (expecting me to say "a child of Christ"), and I would say, "A guy lying on the couch, getting ready to go blind and maybe die." This came from the mouth of a dyed-in-the-wool, career church kid who had been through four and a half years of Bible college and who had helped hundreds of youth and adults through the last ten years of ministry. In my pain, I learned that all my education and experience in ministry was not for me but for others. It was not as if the power I was showing and helping others understand wasn't *for me*. I had spent more time helping other people with their relationship with God and had simply forgotten about the time I should have been spending with Him to get to know His heart.

Holy Crap Moment

Are you spending more time trying to help others with their walk with God than you are seeking God yourself? You can go on for a long time with this mentality, but when the crap happens in life, you will see the deficit you have created. Stop right now and carve out some time each day to get to know Jesus better. Schedule reading your Bible and maybe writing down your thoughts in a journal. Also, learning to just be quiet so that God can speak to you is very important.

Take a Moment

_____

_____

_____

_____

During the "lifestyle of pain," people can lose hope of being healed, and they can go into management mode. They may start to weigh the options of being on destructive medication or not and whether the effects of treatment are worth the problems

> I had spent more time helping other people with their relationship with God and had simply forgotten about the time I should have been spending with Him to get to know His heart.

these drugs may cause elsewhere in the body. I can remember making fun of the commercials on TV that talked about a drug designed to help with one physical condition but gave you seven more as side-effects! They would say something like, "Take this drug to help with your vision, but side-effects include chronic diarrhea, hives, hair falling out, lower back pain, and migraine headaches daily." I never thought in all my life that I would be taking some of those same drugs.

When I was on 80 mg of Prednisone a day, I was working the averages in my mind as to how long I could be on this drug at this dose and if it was worth saving my eye for the destruction of my other organs. I was weighing the benefits against the risks when I was taking Cytoxan, knowing that there was a one-in-four chance that, by taking it, I could get bladder cancer. Even in typing these words for you to read, I cannot describe the times of despair, desolation, and heartbreak that come from this stage of pain.

The third stage is the aftermath of pain. This is the phase of pain I am living in now. I still have my eye but have had to adjust the function of my life because of the damage to the retina caused by massive inflammation. I basically have 20/400 vision in my left eye from the years of my immune system rotting my eye away. I am blessed to still have my eye, and I have good peripheral vision in it, but it is definitely not at 100 percent yet, and that is a type of handicap for me. I am still believing in full restoration because of what God told me in the Bible: "By His wounds, I was (already) healed and made whole."[17] We don't have to settle for less than wholeness, and in this stage there may be some adapting, but like

---

[17] 1 Peter 2:24

Peter, we keep our focus on Jesus and His faithfulness to us. Nothing is impossible for God.

I understand that there were more extreme things that could have happened to me, such as the removal of my eye, and I have had to only temporarily modify my life to accommodate my current physical condition. Also, because of the type of disease I had, the doctors said I could have eventually become blind and had to have both eyes removed, if the condition had wanted to attack the other good eye. I also know that what I went through is nothing compared to the things that others have had to endure in their lives, ranging from cancer to lupus to all sorts of physical or even mental disease.

The aftermath of pain can go in many different directions because everyone's outcome is generally different. I have always had a strong relationship with Jesus, and I know that this experience has enhanced my ability to empathize with people and the fallout of sickness or disease of all kinds in their lives. For example, maybe you had a limb amputated, and your aftermath is learning things all over again with your body and your new prosthetic, not to mention learning how to cope with the emotional stress of losing a physical part of you. Maybe you are dealing with severe emotional issues from hurts or pains from your past, and your aftermath is trying not to let the pains of your past bleed into your current relationships.

My aftermath was damage in my left eye so great that I currently only have peripheral vision. Occasionally, lingering thoughts try to work their way into my mind that the disease I had would come back some day to finish its work. But I know that is the devil, trying to drive me into that corner again with fear and empty threats, so I cast those thoughts down and refuse to entertain them. Sometimes, winning the battle in our thoughts wins the battle over our circumstances too. Here's where knowing that Jesus already took all our sicknesses away and overcame the world, depriving it of power to harm us,[18] will help us to maintain the upper hand in every situation through Christ.

There is one fact that runs through each of these examples, as well as others that I have not even shared. It's the simple fact that while there is professional help for any physical disease or mental sickness we have, if we don't have a connection to Jesus and allow His influence in our lives, it will be too hard to have *complete* success in any of these aftermaths of pain. Complete success is happens when you not only overcome something and get through it but you also recognize that the things you go through happen in order to make you stronger and help other people walk through their difficult times.

This may sound strange, but because of what I have gone through, I have a new respect for God and the place of His church body in my life. Maybe painful experiences *make room* in our lives for God and His people. It's not that He puts bad stuff on us, but He will mercifully use the devil's destruction to bring something really solid and foundational into our lives. My personal and church family was the form of Christ I needed during my time of testing. I cannot even dream what it would have been like to go through my situation without my church friends to help lift me up and encourage me to keep going. It was really strange for me; it wasn't as if I had a *constant* stream of encouragement from the

---

[18] John 16:33

church body, but it ALWAYS came at the right time. A church member would call me to see how I was doing, or a check would arrive in the mail for $1,000 from church people so I could make my house payment and not lose my house. I know the nights of lying in bed, wide awake, wondering how I was going to make the house payment or pay off the ridiculous medical bills that continued to come in daily.

I am starting to cry while typing this because I cannot put into words, really, what the church meant to me while I was going through all those painful days and nights of my journey. Their care and faithfulness has really birthed a drive and purpose in me to write this book and to make sure that I am a blessing to everyone around me. I know what it's like to be so deep in your crap that you think you are never going to see the light of day again.

The aftermath can also go in the direction of even deeper pain and anger, especially at God, where you wonder why you had to go through your struggle. I cannot explain why some people are healed and some are not. I cannot say why I had to go through those years of pain and why I had to come so close to losing my eye. I cannot explain why some people live a life of excellence in service to others, as my mother-in-law did, and then die of such a terrible disease as Lou Gehrig's. What you need to settle in your heart in the aftermath of pain is an understanding and realization of our eternity. We need to see our lives through the eyes of eternity. If we cannot see the length of our eternal existence, then we will get hung up on the outcomes of disease in this life, regardless of how severe those outcomes may be. I can say I have a better understanding of my eternity now that I have gone through my eye situation.

I now realize I am the sum total of all my experiences in this life, good and bad. As a follower of Christ, my central focus in life is helping others understand the importance of making a choice to follow Jesus here on this earth. The key is my attitude while looking back on crap that happens. When I focus on finding what I learned and how God walked with me through a trial rather than just on how I survived, then I can make the best of what happened to me so it can be gold for others. I trust God to hear all my prayers, and I will trust that He has a better plan for me than I could ever imagine for myself. I have learned to keep my eyes on Him through struggles of life, whether instant deliverance comes or I walk all the way through some crap. Either way, I will keep my focus on Christ and believe that I am His loved child that He will never abandon in any circumstance. That same resolve and peace can be yours if you only reach out to God from wherever you are.

What I am basically saying is that you need to be doing something to make a difference in this life–not just to make people feel better but also to find a relationship with Jesus that goes beyond your pain and questions to a place of speaking your heart to Him and then trusting Him to take care of the rest.

Chapter 12
When Pain Has Value

What is it with a traffic accident? In Colorado, there is an epidemic of "gawker traffic" that occurs whenever there are any kind of flashing lights on the side of the road. I am a true believer that some people (although they won't say it) are looking for as much blood and guts as possible when they see the red and blue lights of any kind of emergency vehicle. It really is interesting to think about what people would do if they actually did see something gruesome on the side of the road and had to mentally process it. I think when people see an accident, they are thinking a few things: They may want to see if they know anyone involved in the incident because they genuinely care. Maybe they are thanking God that it wasn't them, or they want to see the level of destruction involved so they have a juicy story when they get to the office.

I say all these things because I believe that seeing pain and destruction in a person's life can evoke some of those same emotions of curiosity in the people around that person. Maybe people around him or her react based on how well they know the person affected by pain. I know that, in a positive way, my sickness has really challenged my parents, my sister, and my wife in their faith and belief in God's grace and power. People may also ask how a person is doing just so they can have the inside scoop when other people ask how that person is doing. When they are talking to the person in pain, they are thinking, if only subconsciously, "I sure am glad I am not going through what that person is." During the years I was sick, I encountered every one of those types of people in conversations. I know that people were watching Yolanda and me, from the myriad of doctors reviewing my case and looking into my eye to people in our neighborhood to friends and family in the church. I am not looking down or talking bad about those people looking at me in any of the ways I identified; I am just saying that it's a fact that people will look at you and your life when you go through pain.

I really want this book to be able to help people on all levels of pain and crap that they go through in life. I firmly believe that crap happens in life, and we have all kinds of opportunities to help others and to let Jesus do something more amazing in the bad times than in the good. When people are looking at you and the life you are living in pain, God has just allowed you to influence and affect the path of their life in a greater way than you could ever imagine. Always remember that it is your decision if you want what you're going through to count for something and to matter to other people or if you just want to turtle up and go into survival mode with your pain.

Holy Crap Moment:

I remember what it felt like to have an immense desire to remove myself from the world and not communicate with anyone when I was dealing with my eye condition, including having thoughts of suicide. Today, don't let what you are dealing with only AFFECT you. Choose today to get mileage out of your situation. Reach out to someone else you know who is going through something and love on them. Send them a card, pray for them, have coffee with them—and this is the key: DON'T talk about what you are going through. Purpose to talk about something positive and encouraging with them. (You weren't expecting this challenge, were you?)

Take a Moment

_____

_____

_____

_____

Survival mode is the automatic reaction to a painful situation, but remember that your initial gut reaction to any painful situation is usually not the right one, no matter what you're getting ready to say, think, or do. I cannot remember one time in my life when I *reacted* to something and it turned out well or helped anyone. In fact, it usually made me look stupid and reactive in that situation. When I stepped back, evaluated my situation, listened to God's promptings, and then ACTED on whatever was happening, I always did my best to make the most out of the situation for myself and for others around me.

Holy Crap Moment:

I am starting this HC Moment with a rhetorical question: have you ever reacted to a situation and then regretted it? We can only learn from situations that were painful, including our problematic reactions to things, and try to be better. Because of my relationship with God, I have the ability to make good decisions—not that I always WILL. Let this book and this moment be your opportunity to make a good decision in the face of your next painful situation. I have faith that you will handle it better next time.

Take a Moment

_____

_____

_____

_____

This is not just you programming yourself to do the right thing when people around you are looking at your life. It takes effort on your part, but it also takes the power of God in your life to do this. In the Bible, Philippians 4:13 (BSB) says, "I can do all things through Christ who strengthens me." It still says that it's me doing the things, but it is the power of Christ in my life that gives me the ability to live a life that is not only pleasing to Him but also encouraging to the people around me.

There is one key thing to remember here: negative circumstances in life can be supernatural and incredible growing experiences if you allow them to be. I can truly say that I have not always done everything right and had a correct *action* for every situation without any *reactions*. When I came home from the eye doctor's office with reports of their growing inclination to remove my eye, I was RIPE with negative reactions, mentally and verbally—out of my mouth! If I didn't have my eye removed, there was a possibility I could go completely blind and a probability I would be on medication for the rest of my life because of my overactive

140

immune system. This book, written through many prayers, is for you to read and learn from my mistakes and also for you to learn something about the principles of not just going through crap and surviving but, in some way, looking forward to those moments as growing experiences.

There are some things to remember about living your life in front of people because they will be watching you and how you react to your painful situation. I have learned from my experiences that there were more opportunities to be a light, and even to help others, when I was sick and going through my pain than there have been when I have been well. I would never recommend sickness over health, but I can say that one is not better than the other when it comes to God's getting glory or our learning from experiences in order to have a better perspective on life. I know I am now more sensitive to others' pain and crap because I went through something out of the ordinary. Perhaps God is just putting more people in my path to help because He knows that I can just listen, or I can know how to pray for people going through something tragic and painful in their lives. I am a firm believer that it is probably a bit of both.

I mentioned this earlier in the book, but I don't think it can be said enough: the times I felt the best going through my pain were when I was not thinking about my crap but instead helping other people. Maybe it was

> The times I felt the best going through my pain were when I was not thinking about my crap but instead helping other people.

counseling people not to quit but rather to go on for one more day, or maybe it was hosting a person Yolanda and I were just loving on who needed a place to stay at night because of some poor decisions he or she was making. I really believe I have become less judgmental of people and of their reaction to the painful situations in their lives than I used to be. I think of people who watched my life as a pastor *before I got sick* and how simplistically I told them, "just do these five things, and you will be better." In the midst of my sickness, however, I tried to do those five things, and it didn't work the way it was supposed to. God was still on the throne; I was still a follower of Him, but I was not experiencing power for myself, which I grew up believing I would see. I believe the problem was that I was not receiving from God's undeserved goodness toward me and His gracious willingness to heal me physically, –simply because that's His loving nature, but I was trying to **do** one thing to **get** something else. It came down to me believing that I was lacking something God had, and I needed to convince Him, through my actions, in order to make Him take action. This is wrong thinking and will only lead to being let down, not by God but by our own actions with wrong motivations.

It is interesting for me to look back on the "eyeball years" because I really feel God was working on my empathy for people more than He was working on my belief in Him while I was going through the worst of my eye situation. I want to state it again because I think this concept is so important for a person following Christ: God was working on my empathy for people more than He was working on my belief in Him. Now, to a "career Christian," this can sound terrible. But I know that if I tell people I love Jesus more than anything in my life, but I can't have empathy for people, give to the needy, help the poor, take care of widows and orphans, or just simply love people who are making bad decisions in life–as I do sometimes–then my relationship with Jesus is a lie.

Holy Crap Moment:

If you call Jesus the main guide for your life, then evaluate how that relationship translates to people who are hurting, lost, dying, or broken. If we are quicker to judge than we are to help, then we are not acting like Christ. People who are broken in this world don't need more people telling them they are broken. They need someone who will help pick up the pieces and encourage them to start again. Be that someone!

Take a Moment

_____

_____

_____

_____

I know that God had me evaluating not only my actions with people who were watching what I did while in pain but also the things I said and whether they brought glory to Him or were just a human reaction to people's painful situations. When I say, "People watching what we do in pain," I mean we can automatically equate that with the things we *do* and forget that we also have words and attitudes that are being watched as well. If we will look for people that we can help when we go through crap, we will be able to help the course of their lives and also feel like we have a purpose greater than just waiting for the other shoe to drop when we are sick or in pain.

Knowing that others are watching us in our pain can also extract a greater desire in us to get the most out of our pain. When we go through something crappy in life, we are met with a decision to either complain and assess whether we think we deserve what we are getting or to use our experience to bring hope and light to somebody else. When we do the former and complain, we are missing the point of painful situations. I really believe that pain is not meant to show us what we haven't done to make God happy but an opportunity to learn something about ourselves that we would have never known if everything was going well in life. In the Bible, Paul talks about our infirmities and taking pleasure in them.

> "Most gladly therefore will I rather glory in my infirmities, that the power of Christ may rest upon me. Therefore I take pleasure in infirmities, in reproaches, in necessities, in persecutions, in distresses for Christ's sake: for when I am weak, then am I strong."[19]

Please understand that infirmities can encompass more than just physical pain. They can also be mental, spiritual, or emotional in nature.

Holy Crap Moment

Infirmities are more than just physical sickness in life. When we realize that sickness is more than just how we feel and can be emotional or spiritual as well, we put ourselves on a path of complete healing on all levels. Take a Moment right now and think

---

[19] 2 Cor 12:9 (AMP)

of some ways that you are dealing with an infirmity that is not physical. This can be an emotional hurt from your past or maybe some form of manipulation that you experienced in life that is just easier to block out than to remember. Ask God right now to begin a process of healing these areas of your life. Today is the day you begin to let things go and let God meet you at your point of need. The only way you can learn from these painful situations is to not let the crap of yesterday keep you from learning and growing stronger. The only one to stop or start a growth process in your life is you. Choose life today!

Take a Moment

_____

_____

_____

_____

If we are not looking to GET the most out of pain and hurt in our lives, then it will TAKE the most out of us. Think of this example to help illustrate this principle; I call it the "Escalators of Life." When things are going well in life, it's like a set of stationary stairs that we are climbing. We see a destination at the top of the staircase and can see ourselves getting closer to the top. I see myself living a life of getting closer to God each day and hopefully becoming more and more like Him. Escalators on that walk with God are the moments when we feel as if things are going backward in life. For instance, if I keep walking at the same pace when the down escalator starts, then I will slowly go down in the progression of my life.

When I say we need to make the most of the downward opportunities in life, I am saying that we need to see it as a time in our lives that we can work out our walk more. People will be watching if we let the escalator of life pull us down and cause us to lose hope and stop walking altogether.

Walking faster in life occurs when we work on helping others in the down times of our life. It is when we make a point to spend more time in prayer and Bible reading (two things that I now regret that I didn't do much of when I was sick and would advise others to do when going through pain in life). The down times in life help us to respect and appreciate the normal climb of life without the stairs moving. The "fun" thing is that, through the stairs and downward-moving escalator of life, people are going to be watching how you react to those times. They will be asking you what you are doing to not merely get through them but to actually see success while pain is happening in your life.

In my own experience, I saw the church body come in, pick me up when I was ready to stop climbing, put me on their back, and help me climb when I was ready to quit. There is an enormous amount of power and help in being involved in a church body. I can remember a Sunday morning when Pastor Marilyn Hickey asked for people who wanted healing for eyes to stand for prayer. I raised my hand and stood up in the balcony

> In my own experience, I saw the church body come in, pick me up when I was ready to stop climbing, put me on their back, and help me climb when I was ready to quit.

of our church where I was working that Sunday morning. Another friend and pastor on staff, Jill, saw me raise my hand from the floor of the sanctuary. She could have turned and prayed with many other people who had their hand raised downstairs but chose to come up to the balcony and pray with me. We have been friends for many years and on staff together, but that simple moment was a highlight of my sick years and is a perfect example of the love I felt being a part of a group of believers in Jesus that was bigger than just myself. There were so many of those kinds of above and beyond moments in my life connected to the church body that when I think about it, even now, I get overwhelmed.

The love and support I felt when I was not able to go on is what motivates me to pray for people who are in need of prayer, a listening ear, or just emotional support. The church was my form of Jesus when I didn't completely feel the presence of God in my life during the crap I was going through. I know there were people watching these things happen around me, and it encouraged them to go on, be more committed to the church, or seek God on a higher level than they normally would have.

When my nephew Jalen was in grade school, he took me by surprise with an essay he wrote for school about who his hero was in this life (and someone he looks up to). He picked me because of my eye situation and because he saw the strength of God working through my life. I read that essay and know that it was not my power but Christ working through me, through a loving church, through my family, and through my wife who would not let me quit. I can say without a doubt that God has used my painful situation for my good and for the good of others.

Holy Crap Moment

Just take a second, stop your life for a minute, and appreciate one thing that is good. Times of appreciation can help when the depreciation in life happens, and you can seem lost and without strength to go on. After my crap years, I now try to be diligent to appreciate what I have and where I feel God has brought me. Those times of appreciation are as markers on the road of life to help you not lose yourself when the road gets rough and times get dark. Also realizing that people will watch and can be encouraged by what you have walked through can be a reason to rejoice in the situations you have had to endure.

Take a Moment

_____

_____

_____

_____

When people are watching what you are going through, remember that there may be a time when the tables are turned, and you may need to provide help to them in some way. I really believe that has become a core truth to me in my walk with God. I always want to be praying for people and helping them find answers to problems in their lives.

I am confident that when people are in pain, you are more open to answers to questions you have about trouble in your life. That openness is possibly because what you have been doing is not working or the things you have committed to in your life are not bringing the results you want. Maybe you are a "good vibrations" kind of person, and you are relying on positive thoughts from others to encourage you. Maybe you are just trying to out think the situation you are in and are using what you know and see in the physical realm to explain a pain that definitely seems other-worldly. Whatever the case may be, I want to be an ambassador of the Love of Jesus and help give a spiritual and heavenly perspective on your pain and what God can do in the middle of despair. This book is not just about helping people feel better about comfortably going through pain. It is about my sharing my power source and the only real hope I have to share with people. Without Him, just in my own flesh, I am not good enough or smart enough, nor do I have the kind of answers I get from knowing Jesus. It is a real, vibrant, and practical relationship with Jesus that is the answer.

When people see me go through something in life, I want them to see that I appreciate the personal aspect of what Jesus teaches me when I take time out of my day and spend time with Him, but it's also the power of the body of Christ. There is something special when people who love Jesus more than anything else in life get together to worship Him, receive Bible-based teaching, and are given an opportunity to share the things God is doing in their lives for the enrichment of others I know there are doubters out there as far as the local church is concerned, but I can say that I would probably not be here and would have killed myself without the prayers and encouragement of my church.

We all want to think we are strong enough to make it on our own, but I just don't think it's true. If you are watching me through reading this book and reading the story of the worst and most painful thing I have ever dealt with emotionally, physically, and spiritually, then know that I am a product of a godly family, a church that supported me, and a God who loved me even though I thought, at times, it was more important to have the title of Pastor than it was to be a man of God. When I say I want people to watch me, then I want to be the best reflection of Christ I can be, because He is all I am and the best thing that ever came from me. I am still flawed, and I need to work on my life, but with Christ working through me, I know I am just beginning to learn amazing things about who I am in this world and how I will affect it for the glory of God.

Chapter 13
The Dos and Don'ts

Maybe you are reading this book and are a pre-pain person (meaning you have not yet gone through a life-changing situation associated with pain, but you will), or you are watching a person go through pain. I believe that most people who are not going through pain have the best of intentions, but I am writing this to help people understand there are certain things that can be said or withheld to help the person going through pain get through it better and with more help from people around them.

I would advise that the first and most important thing to never do say to person in pain is, "I know what you are going through." No one person can know exactly how another person feels about a certain type of pain with which he or she is dealing. Even brothers and sisters in the same family have a different experience that will cause them each to deal with pain in a different way. I really believe that people who say they know what you are going through have the best of intentions, but to the person in pain it can feel as if they are saying, "What you are dealing with is nothing worse than what I have also experienced." Even though that may be true on all levels, the person in pain does not want to hear this type of thing. The best thing to do for someone who is going through pain is to pray for them and to listen to them. Prayer is supernatural support for them for which they may not even be able to ask.

I used to think that, unless someone says that he is victorious in a situation, he is doomed until he can utter those magical words.

You may read that sentence and disagree with what I just said, but I am speaking from experience and from a Pentecostal, Charismatic, Jesus-lovin' background of faith. There are no words in the English language to express what I experienced from being prayed for by the Body of Christ. It was almost as if a veil was lifted on my understanding about the power of prayer for others. Experiencing that prayer support is what inspired me to do a Friend Prayer Day on Tuesdays on my social networking site and to take requests for prayer from friends. It is what changed me from being a person who used to say to people in church, "I will pray for you" without following through to being a person who, if I say, "I will pray," I do.

Listening is another thing I am working on, even though I have gone through my own crap in life. This is not easy for people like me who love to help solve people's problems. I don't like leaving things undone if there is something I know I can do. My personality is not inherently one of a good listener, and it takes supernatural discipline for me to be a good godly listener. That is why I am still learning how to do this excellently. Listening to someone who is dealing with pain is supernatural because you are not trying to be one of the people in their lives trying to solve their problem like doctors, psychologists, therapists, financial consultants, etc. All those people play important roles in getting through crap in life, but it can get VERY overwhelming when you have so many voices in your life trying to tell you what to do to get through your pain. Caring and listening to someone can be just as amazing and wonderful to them as getting financial advice or having a doctor diagnose a problem and put together an action plan to get healthy again would be.

Please don't think you are going to have all the answers for people in pain. Actually, one of the greatest things you can give someone going through pain is what I would call silent proximity. Just be around them, love them, and listen to them. Don't listen so that you can

Caring and listening to someone can be just as amazing and wonderful to them as getting financial advice or having a doctor diagnose a problem and put together an action plan to get healthy again would be.

have an antidote for their situation, but just listen for the sake of listening. As a guy, I know this is a difficult process because of our "listen then fix" mentality. But we need to discipline ourselves around people who just need someone to be there without having all the answers on how to fix something.

It is always paramount to remember that health in a person's life is more than mental, physical, or emotional. It is also having healthy relationships with people who will believe the best for you when you have no strength to believe for yourself. It's having encouraging, spiritually-minded friends who will pray prayers for you that you can't pray on your own. I believe these are important elements to a strong walk with God that are not learned until trouble hits in life or problems occur in your life or the lives of your loved ones. There are lessons that cannot be learned if pain is not present in a person's life.

Probably the most important thing that you can do when you see someone go through pain in life, if you are a follower of Christ, is to obey the promptings of the Holy Spirit to do things for them. You have no idea how beautiful the perfect timing of God in someone's life can be when you are obedient to speak an encouraging word to that person or when you just let him or her know you are thinking about that one and praying for the best. They may have been a whisper away from giving up when your word of hope and encouragement came to them. There were so many times this happened for me when I was sick that I cannot even count them. When you are sick, you really realize the power of words in your life–words that can lift up and encourage or words that can tear down and bring more pain.

You could also give a monetary gift to help pay bills if they have medical issues. Yolanda and I received some amazing financial gifts during the years I was sick and out of work. If I showed you a list of the people who gave us money alongside their modest bank accounts, it would surprise you how many didn't really even have the money to give but wanted to be a blessing. Many times we think, "If I only had more money, I would give it to someone in need." The problem with money is that there is never enough a person can acquire before he or she feels like it's enough. Giving money can seem like a shallow reminder in a book like this, but until you have been under the stress and load of medical bills in some way, you will never understand what a monetary gift can do for a person in physical need. It can provide the hope to go on for one more day and not give up.

One thing that is important to do with someone going through pain is just to spend time with them without talking about what they are going through. This sounds like avoidance, but when you are going through something painful, it is possibly on your mind twenty-four hours a day, seven days a week. To have a reprieve from your situation and do something fun, such as going for coffee, and not have to talk about the situation can be very helpful for a person going through pain. Don't bring up the person's situation. This might help the person realize that his or her life has the ability to be normal again. I can remember days when I was so sick that I thought I would never be off prednisone and that I would always be taking drugs for my eye at 9:00 a.m. and 9:00 p.m. every day of my life. Because I was on immuno-suppressant drugs, I was not supposed to be out in the sun (because you have a greater risk of skin cancer while taking them). So I thought I would never be able to be out in the sun again. When you can just go out with the person going through pain and just be normal, it is like an oasis in the middle of a horrendous and never-ending desert of pain.

Holy Crap Moment

Below, you'll see three Holy Crap Moments, in no particular order, with action points for helping to contact and HELPFULLY connect with someone in their pain. These are not just a step by step of helping to love on someone; they're just suggestions to connect in a loving and caring way.

Step 1: Be a Good listener

Think of someone today who is going through a painful situation. Contact them, see if you can go do something with them, and make it a point not to talk about what they are going through unless they bring it up. This is where it is important to be a good listener and not just a nervous talker.

Take a Moment

_____

_____

_____

_____

When we watch people going through pain, we can think there must be something huge and amazing that is about to happen in their lives as a result of their trial that will be a benefit to them and others. Just being a friend and doing things with them that show they are more than what they are going through is huge in the life of a person dealing with personal crap.

Something not to do, even though you may have the best intentions, is give the person going through crap the "next best thing" in supplements or medical clippings from something you saw on the internet. I know this can be a touchy point to make, and I definitely had my share of people give me *stuff* through the years that I was sick. There was a point, however, when the amount of advice I got from people about my disease just became overwhelming. Again, I knew their hearts were in the right place in giving me the things they did, but it just felt so overwhelming—and not in a good way. Believe me when I tell you that people who are going through a sickness are already looking for alternatives to the treatment they are currently undergoing and will already be asking for this type of information from personal and professional sources.

Please remember that I am only talking from my personal experience with pain, and these points are to let you know that the people you are around who are going through pain may possibly be feeling this way as well. Everyone is going to deal with and react to pain differently, and each one will have individual responses to pain.

If you are a follower of Christ, the most important thing you can do is stay attentive in your prayer life to the needs of people who you know are dealing with crap. I know I have mentioned this more than once in the book, but after going through my own form of pain, I can say that I am now more sensitive to people going through crap in life and will pray for them. It is also helpful to let people for whom you are praying know that you lifted them up in prayer and at what time of the day. I can remember countless times when people sent me an email or text or left me a message, saying that at 3:30 p.m. that day they were praying for me. I would think back to that exact time and remember that, at that exact moment, I was thinking about giving up and maybe killing myself but decided not to.

Prayer can seem like such an insignificant thing in the life of a believer in Christ, because it is so readily available to them, but it is invaluable to people who are going through pain who can't pray prayers for themselves. You will never know how important prayer is until you feel like you can't say the things that need to be said to have peace in your mind and life. I had so many people, some whom I had never met before, along with a wonderful church body of people at Orchard Road Christian Center, who prayed all the prayers I needed in order to make it through and to be typing this book today to encourage everyone who reads it. I also had family and friends who prayed all the strategic prayers I couldn't pray for myself and my wife. If you are one of the people who prayed for me through the years of my sickness, then you have a part in this book, touching lives, making a difference to people going through crap in life, and giving hope to the hopeless. Yolanda and I thank you from the bottom of our hearts.

Holy Crap Moment

Step 2: Contact someone and say a prayer for them

Take some time right now and pray for someone you know who is going through something in life and who needs your prayers. Then call or text them and tell them you are praying for them. It doesn't need to be something long and religious. Actually, the shorter and more to the point it is, the better. Sometimes when we pray long prayers, we get lost in the formality of saying words and get away from the things that need to be said. Here is an example of a great short prayer you can pray: "Jesus, thank You for being with _____. Let them know You are with them and helping in the situation beyond what they see in the physical moment. I thank You for loving them, and bless them today in Jesus name. Amen."

Take a Moment

_____

_____

_____

_____

Finally, the last thing you want to do is lose contact with the person who needs to have your friendship and prayer. We can get so busy with our own lives and lose contact with people who need to possibly have a regular touch from us. I am sure this is never intentional, but that doesn't really matter to the person in need. We have so many technological devices in our lives that can help us remember all kinds of things. Use those devices to remind yourself to reach out and touch people in need. I have a smartphone that can do many things, and I have a list in my Notes section that is dedicated to praying for people who I know are in need. Effort is all that is needed to make sure you don't lose contact with people who need to be lifted up when they can't lift themselves or their circumstances up to God.

For many people, these are the moments of spiritual life-support. Your support is not going to carry that person forever but will provide the ability for outside systems (your support, prayers, and contacts) to keep them going so they can recover and heal. You're giving them the ability to believe things that they cannot on their own–for a season. You're giving them an emotional rest from the pain of life in order to recover, to heal, and to move on. It might even be physically doing something for them that is above and beyond a phone call, coffee, or prayer.

Holy Crap Moment

Step 3: If needed, be a "life-support" friend

Is there someone in your life right now who needs you to be his or her life-support? You may need to think about what you can do beyond just saying a prayer for someone and just listening to them. There were times when Yolanda and I felt as if we needed to do more than just verbally encourage and listen. Sometimes we need to do something with our hands that is meaningful and will encourage someone going through crap in their life. This is the most difficult step because, many times, people don't want your help, but I think it is still important to offer to be there. We were made to encourage one another and to lift one another up when we fall. Give the same kind of love that you would want if you were the one dealing with the pain, because someday it might just be you.

Take a Moment

_____

_____

_____

_____

What an awesome responsibility we have to each other to lift one another up when we are going through troubled times in life! I have said it before, and I will say it again: the church has never been more important in a person's life than when he or she is dealing with a tragedy or some type of crap that can seem overwhelming. If you are not a part of a Bible-believing church, I encourage you, again, to get involved in one and to ask God what things you can do to lift up the people in that Body of Christ. We were created to have fellowship with Jesus but also with each other. We were created to share that touch we all need, because pain and suffering in life is inevitable but so is the strength and power of Christ in tandem with the body of believers. I want the people around me to know that they can rely on Jesus, *and* that they can trust that I will do my part to lift them up when they need it.

Chapter 14
Don't Let Despair Stop Your Giving

When you go through something painful in life, I believe the times that you are able to get away from the tormenting thoughts stand out because they are times that help you keep your sanity. In the middle of all the crap that Yolanda and I were dealing with, the strongest times for us happened when we were reaching out to other people and "giving out of our poverty," literally and figuratively. We had people who came into our lives for us to take care of and reach out to, even in the middle of the darkest time of need in our own lives.

On one night, we got a call at 2:30 a.m. from a girl to whom we had been ministering. We drove thirty-five minutes across town to pick her up at a party and found she had locked herself in the bathroom because she was drunk and afraid she was going to be raped. I can remember Yolanda and myself driving to pick her up and not even thinking of the excruciating pain in my eye, because I was only concerned about getting to her and helping her in the middle of her pain. I was not even thinking about or worried about the car coming toward us, driving on the wrong side of the highway in the median, while we drove to pick her up (true story).

There were a few things that happened when we were reaching out to others. For one, we would stop obsessing about ourselves. I have mentioned this numerous times: when you get sick, you get self-centered. Sickness is the catalyst for worrying and thinking only about yourself and your needs or your lack. I believe our character is forged as a result of difficult situations, not pleasant ones. Think about that statement for a moment. We have been trained to live for the epic moments of glory and for those feel good days. We are not told or programmed to look forward to painful situations in life. Those painful days, however, are opportunities to enhance or even build character in us because they help us see what we lack in our own abilities, and we begin to see God's power make up the difference. You begin to do and say things that are beyond you and your own thought process because you have Jesus in your heart and as your guide, helping to direct your words and actions.

Paul, who was an amazing man in the Bible, talks about being content in all things. I used to think that was one of the stupidest sections of the Bible and actually wished that the pages in my Bible would support sharpie marker ink so that I could cross it out. Of course I am kidding, but why would anyone want to have pain in his life, and why would anyone want to say he gloried in his suffering? Isn't suffering, by definition, not a good thing? I really believe Paul had found a perspective that escapes many in life, which is that pain is as inevitable as life but our reaction to painful situations is not. Part of that holy reaction in pain is not just about yourself but also considering how you can reach out to others around you in the midst of pain and crap in your life. The thing that is so amazing about having Jesus in the crap of your life is that He has the ability to teach, to train, and to make you a better person. If you don't believe in God, you will live life trying to avoid the inevitable in life, pain. Or you will run to other avoidance techniques, which are only detours that bring you right back to where the pain began.

When I turn on the TV, I don't see commercials and shows that are about finding pain in life and the wonderful benefits of going through difficult situations. I do see people on talk shows who have gone through terrible situations, and the audience just sits and listens with wonder and amazement, and they think to themselves, "Wow! I'm glad that wasn't me!" They are not thinking, "Wow! What an amazing lesson in learning who you really are." Followers of Christ should not shy away from painful situations, but embrace them as a chance to stand out and really show what a relationship with Jesus can do. We want to consider not just ourselves, but we want to reach out to people in need. The best testimony to me is someone dealing with their own crap but finding time and energy to bless someone else in their life.

Here's another point about reaching out to people when you are sick yourself: when people know you are going through a painful situation in your life, and you still want to reach out and help them, it is an amazing thing. Until I got sick, I didn't know what it was like to sit in a room at the Arthritis Clinic receiving my own

> The best testimony to me is someone dealing with their own crap but finding time and energy to bless someone else in their life.

Remicade IV drip to try and stop my eye from rotting out of my head and at the same time offer to pray for another person sitting in that same room who had a terminal disease that they are only able to manage with drugs. There are no words in the English language that could explain how I felt at those moments. They were some of the most humbling, life-changing, and life-giving moments I've ever known.

At the same time, I was dealing with my own relationship with Jesus and wondering if I really believed all the things I was praying for them. Both to them and to myself, it was true proof that God was working through my sickness and touching someone's life in a way that that person would probably not accept from someone who felt well and was not really going through anything in life. God loved the people around me so much that he even patiently worked around my thoughts of doubt to minister to these people I came in contact with. He loves you so much that he put a verse in the Bible that says, "Neither height nor depth, nor anything else in all creation, will be able to separate us from the love of God that is in Christ Jesus our Lord."[20] Now THAT is some powerful love, and you have access to it anytime you want!

There are countless examples in the Bible of people being delivered from painful situations but also of people who had to walk through crappy circumstances while keeping their heads up and needing to keep going. Personally, I don't *want* to hear how beneficial pain is or how much I can show Christ's power because His strength is made perfect in my weakness. As someone who seeks to follow Christ every day, many times I can get just as mad as anyone else and say some of the same things and react in the exact same ways. This is not said by someone who has only observed it happening to others, but by someone who sometimes

---

[20] Rom 8:39 (NIV)

still reacts to painful situations in the same way a non-follower of Christ would.

I hope and pray you hear my transparency in these statements. I know that my relationship with Jesus is strong, but it's just that my flesh gets in the way sometimes when I am in the fire with painful situations. It still does even today. One of the greatest misconceptions of being a follower of Christ is that, once you give Jesus control of your life, everything gets easier. It is not about everything being easier, but that there is now a place to take your pain and someone to lean on when you deal with the inevitable crap of life.

I learned a very important but painful lesson while going through this journey with my eye: I am no better than anyone else on his or her journey of knowing who Jesus is to them. I want my relationship with Jesus to be something that people who don't have peace in their lives really want. The whole focus of a believer in Christ should be to see life for the ups and downs that it is and then have such a close relationship with Jesus in spite of that that other people want the relationship you have.

When followers of Christ act and react like others who don't have that same hope and foundation, the relationship we have with Jesus is viewed more as extra rules and regulations you have in your life. Think about this: no one wants rules and regulations in his or her life unless that person knows he or she will benefit from them in some way. Rules and regulations that are viewed as being imposed by Christ are no different. Followers of Christ must be the shining examples of lives lived to touch other people, no matter how you feel or what is going on in your life. Sometimes the problem is that followers of Christ don't feel as if their lives are any better off than anyone else's who is dealing with the crap of life. The truth is that it's way better–because true followers of Christ know where to take that pain and to give those things to Jesus.

The amazing thing about this statement is that a relationship with Jesus and a peace that passes all understanding is only as far away as reaching out to God and saying a quick prayer. Anyone can start that relationship with Jesus to have a foundation of power, strength, and hope in all situations in life.

Holy Crap Moment

Take some time right now and evaluate your relationship with Jesus and His value in your life. If it's not God, who or what do you turn to in life when it really gets bad? Do those other things/people have solutions to the issues you deal with? Do they make things worse? Do they just mask or cover up a deeper issue in your life that you need to deal with? Trusting in God and His ability to help you walk through life can be a game-changer for you. It is also important that you are in a good Bible-believing church with other followers of Christ to help you sort out the details when it gets rough.

Take a Moment

_____

_____

_____

_____

Reaching out to others in need when I have needs myself is the greatest witnessing tool I have as a person who gives Jesus the highest priority in his life. As I think back on my physical circumstances, I had four-plus years to get my crap in order. Instead, at times, I went into survival mode–and I am slightly disappointed in the things I still have to learn. I am, now more than ever, a firm believer that painful situations are the true test of a person and of what they have or haven't learned in their walk with Jesus. The reason I say this is that having Jesus in your heart does not make you less vulnerable to pain.

I believe the ubiquitous nature of pain in the life of every human being is an absolutely perfect opportunity to share the light inside of you. People have been lied to and told that once you ask Jesus into your life to help guide and direct your actions, everything is rainbows and unicorns. Not true. If you could ask Jesus into your life to guide you and make all of life free from pain, then don't you think every person would accept Jesus? Pain in life causes us to need to rely on Jesus and make positive decisions out of that pain.

Too many times, as humans, we make decisions **IN** pain and not **OUT OF** pain. In other words, when I make a decision in pain, I am reacting to the forces around me and am only concerned with how that pain is affecting me and no one else. If I am making decisions out of pain, I am choosing to do things that are not related to the pain going on in my life, but out of the convictions of a heart surrendered to Jesus. If there was no pain for the follower of Christ, then we would not be put in a position to be made better as a person. We would actually be relying on Christ in a selfish way that would be for making our life easier, and an easier life is not necessarily a better life. I don't want the easiest life I can get. I want the *best* life I can get, and Jesus gives me that advantage.

I want to go back to an earlier chapter where I mentioned hurt that people have perceived as coming from God, church, "Christians", etc. Maybe you are still thinking that you can't move beyond a standard that someone set for you in order for you to qualify as a Christian, and you don't want a relationship with Christ. I want you to remember that the whole concept of a relationship with Christ is that it's personal and not based on anything that anyone else has done or will do. Jesus wants to have a relationship with you in which you can talk to Him, rely on Him for direction in life, and help improve the quality of your life in general. Again, I am not promising a lack of pain or struggles but rather a safe place to go when things go wrong in life.

I say all of these things because when you are able to reach out to others in your pain, you are on the road to learning something amazing from your pain. That turns the crap in your life into *holy crap*, a kind of pain that is directly connected to perfecting you as a person. This changes your perspective from staying away from pain to using the painful times of life to make awesome decisions that people around you need. They need to see you handle pain with grace and a determination that is greater than a power of positive thinking CD they picked up at the local bookstore to use to get through life.

I have been a follower of Christ for essentially my whole life, and I believe I have some good principles that God has shown me–especially after four-plus years of being sick–but I know I still have a long way to go in my knowledge of God. It doesn't mean I can't follow Him; it just means that I can never get prideful again and think I know more than anyone else. The only good things I have for people who call me their pastor or even their friend is what I get from Jesus. Being a follower of Christ is about a few simple things: loving others as much as you love yourself (or maybe as much as you should love yourself), offering support to people in their difficulties in life, and offering people eternal life with a caring and loving God Who will not disappoint. Please don't forget that HolyCrapBook.com can be an excellent continuing resource for you and can also be a place to direct other hurting people who need encouragement.

Chapter 15
Answers to Consider

To write this final chapter, I tried to go to a bookstore this morning, located near my house, where I first started writing my book. I pulled up to the location with my laptop in hand and a focus to finish this book. As I was walking up to the entrance, a little kid ran up to the door in front of me and started pulling on it with all her might. I heard her mom say, "No, honey. That door is locked." As I looked up at where the sign should have been, I saw that it was gone; peering into the window, I could see that everything was cleared out of the building. It was a kind of symbol to me that the past is gone. I have many fond memories of sitting in that bookstore, weekend after weekend, writing my story partly as therapy and partly as a promise I had made to myself and God to eventually write a book in my lifetime. I decided to get back in the car and drive up to the mountains. Today, I am at a coffee location in the town of Conifer, Colorado, where my buddy and I usually go after we hike one of our favorite locations. I never really realized it, but this place reminds me of the success God has given me over the devil, his lies for the years I was sick, and his telling me that I would not be able to do the things I enjoy, including hiking.

I was praying on the drive up here and was reminded of something very pertinent to people going through pain. I believe humans are programmed to look at the past when pain hits. We get laser-focused on, "If only things could be like they were in life." The problem with that statement is we don't understand that the future and where we can be in life can be greater than the "good ol' days."

When we persevere, we build strength in our lives that we would never have had without it. I remember the first time my friend Aaron and I hiked the area around this coffee shop. We were sweating and stopping at every switchback, consuming massive amounts of water, and thinking we were on a trek up some 14,000-foot peak, when in reality, we were less than a mile and not more than a couple hundred feet in elevation gain from the trailhead! The persistence of going hiking about every other weekend since that initial ascent helped us master that mountain and start to enjoy the climb. I know God did not make the things happen to me with my eye, but I know what I went through was something that built strength in me to go on and believe in great things for my future.

The bookstore closing and my drive to the mountain coffee shop was just another gentle reminder that the start of my journey is locked and in the past, but the future climbs of life and the things I have learned even since starting to write this book are ahead of me. We all have two decisions in life when pain hits; we can either worry **backward** or pray **forward**. Backward is familiar to us because it is something we experienced, and we have a point of reference of a time without pain. When I pray forward, I decide to look ahead with an expectation of solutions that bring even greater levels of contentment with God leading my life, using a roadmap that I could never access without Him. A fact of hiking that is true in life as well is that maps lead to destinations, but guesses lead to being lost. I trust God much more with my navigation than I do my best guesses in life or worrying about situations that, in reality, I will never be able to control anyway.

So what do you do with this story about a pastor from Colorado whose eye almost rotted out of his head? What do you do with the many lessons that he and his wife learned through five years of family deaths, being on more drugs than a pharmaceutical company, and coming close to suicide and who is still overcoming residual effects of his disease? Useful knowledge is only good when it is used and applied. If you just consider this a "Wow, how about that story!" kind of book, then you probably won't get much out of this, and you're probably moving on to the next non-fiction book of choice. Or the information in this book can provoke you to take the time to slow down and stop to think about where you are in life. Today is the day to consider confident hope as an option in the struggles of life instead of it becoming a residual outcome of despair.

I mentioned it before, and I will mention it again: it is not a matter of *whether* pain will happen in life but a matter of *when*. It is also true that your **decisions** in pain will determine your **destination** after pain. Maybe you just got back from the doctor and the word "idiopathic" came out of your doctor's mouth, and you are still a little stunned. Maybe you are a parent in the middle of life and taking care of a special needs child or spouse, and you have settled in to your routines of life. This book is a reflection of what I went through, combined with basic life principles that I believe God wanted me to share with the world. I made a few mistakes along the way that you can hopefully learn from, but the key thought I want to share is

> Today is the day to consider confident hope as an option in the struggles of life instead of it becoming a residual outcome of despair.

don't give up! I am sure you have heard this statement before, but it is worth repeating when you are in times of despair; the day you give up with first day you fail.

Please hear me. I completely believe in miraculous healing, but I also firmly believe that the God I serve is supremely concerned about the eternal condition of my heart and my dedication to Him, not just the temporary condition of my physical body while I am alive on this earth. I have a much greater view of my eternal existence and the importance of good decisions in life now. I would hope that if you are not a follower of Christ, you would consider a deeper relationship with Jesus and would be willing to turn control of your life over to Him. Just say out loud right now, "Lord Jesus, I want to give You control of my life. I want You in charge of all areas of my life. Show me how to have a deeper relationship with You." There is a power and ability to have hope in the depths of despair that only comes from keeping your eyes on Jesus and what He has to offer. It is a lifeline that can only be accessed by giving God complete control of your life.

If you are a person watching someone go through pain, you don't understand what is happening, and you feel helpless, then know that both of those feelings are absolutely valid, but there are things you can do to let those people know you are there for them. Below, I address a few groups of people to help sum up what I have been saying. You may find a little of yourself in all three of these groups, so be sure to read all three. And don't just read through them as entertainment, but look for areas of your life in which *you* need to make changes, whether you are watching someone in pain or going through crap in your own life.

174

Some people are emotionally or physically healed instantly. The Bible is full of people in this group, and maybe you know some in your life as well. Others have to walk all the way through a painful and uncomfortable situation. My story, and perhaps your own as well, would fit in that second group. Still others get so angry at the organization of church that they try and do it alone with their relationship with God. Then they feel isolated and disconnected from other true believers who can help on so many levels if they can forgive and move on. How many people do you know who fit in this group? If this is you, when was the last time you felt peace in your own heart and mind?

God promises He will never leave or abandon us, but He does not promise that life will always go the way we want it to or that we will never have pain. If you are not a follower of Christ, God can be with you–if you want to have a relationship with Him. Even though I have mentioned, throughout my story, the power and importance of being a part of a group of other followers of Christ, it is still a personal relationship with Jesus. It is the simplest and yet most difficult thing someone can ever do: crying out to God for help and then giving control of life over to Him. Giving Him the priority of time and attending church or picking up a Bible and spending time reading about His love and plan for you. Surrendering thoughts of destruction in favor of constructive thoughts that give solutions to dead ends in life. It can also be difficult to imagine anything normal in life when you feel like there has been so much destruction and no way out for so many years. A walk with Jesus is just that, a walk–putting one foot in front of the other and continuing to move forward. Sometimes the destination can look so far away because of the destruction that we don't even start to move from a place of ill mental or physical health.

I started running about a year ago, and when I was sick, I could never have imagined in a million years that I would be able to run more than eight miles and not pass out! When I talk to people about them starting to run, I say, "If you never start to run as far as you can, you will never be able to run as far as you want." Stop looking at how far it is to go with getting to know Jesus, and just do what you can now. I feel so strongly about you starting this relationship with Jesus that I want to give you a few resources as well as places to start reading the Bible. If you go to HolyCrapBook.com right now and click on "Starting a Relationship with Jesus," there are some great resources for you to get your journey going.

The culture seems to be against the structure of church and people meeting together in a formal setting on a weekly basis, but it really is amazing to be part of a network of people connected to more than just good vibrations or a higher authority but to a God who can hear our cries and who wants to actually have a relationship with us. The God I serve prompted countless friends and family to call, email, and give cards and books to encourage my faith. He prompted them to give money so we would not lose our house and to give lunches, dinners, and boxes of groceries to us, just to name a few things. It was overwhelming how much we felt the love of Christ from people we had known over the years.

The God I serve knew when I would want to kill myself because of my health and, over twenty years ago, had me marry the best woman I have ever met to be the strength I needed until I could once again pray those prayers of power that I used to. I know these thoughts and facts are mostly an opinion from a guy who you have never met or probably even heard of, but I'm telling you that the simple but relevant words of the Bible and the power of God in your life is a *fact*. They have the ability to guide you and help you if you choose to embrace them.

The truth is that if you know you need God, there's not much I need to do to convince you to follow Him. That's just how great I think He is. I do know that there are many who say they love Christ but use hate, condemnation, and fear against people to make their point and call it the love of God. They are abusing the gracious and unconditional true love of God because they don't even know God themselves.

As a follower of Christ, I want to formally apologize for those who have hurt you in the name of Christ. There is no excuse or biblical example for that kind of behavior, and I want to say I am sorry to those of you who have formed an opinion about God based on someone who had falsely followed Him. True Christians who live and love like Jesus did say, "I am not perfect, but that I'm doing my best to listen to what He wants, love like He loves, and then provide opportunities for people to invite Him into their lives and see the power and peace that follows in life, regardless of life's circumstances."

There is something you should know that is not very popular in some church circles. The Bible is not about just making you feel good. It feels much better to sit on the couch and do nothing for my health rather than going for a run or a hike to stay in shape. It feels good to eat chocolate for breakfast, lunch, and dinner, but it doesn't mean it is healthy for me. Every time I pick up and read the Bible, it challenges me to be a better person today than I was last year at this time. Does it mean I always make the right decisions? Absolutely not. But it does mean that I have that map for life I mentioned previously that shows me exactly how to be successful on every level.

An additional thing I want to mention is the false sense of security we can have in life. We buy life, home, medical (even pet) insurance so that we can be taken care of when something in life goes wrong. We have airbags in cars, and we trust that they will deploy at just the right time. We have police and local law enforcement agencies that are one phone call away from coming to our aid in the event of an emergency. We make storm shelters, we wear helmets when we ride our mountain bikes or motorcycles, and we install anti-virus software on our digital devices. This next statement is very important to learn, realize, and understand before you get done reading this book: all the things we do to prevent bad things from happening in our lives give us a sense of control that doesn't really exist. All of this points to one of the best reasons I can give someone for following Christ and committing his or her focus and attention to Him–it's the pure fact that we are not promised tomorrow. Through Christ, though, you can have the promise of eternity.

Problems and bad things have been happening for centuries to much better people than you and me. I am not saying that it's smart not to prepare and have or use the safety measures listed above, but doing those things and expecting never to have anything bad happen to you or thinking you have some kind of safety net to prevent all potential crap in life is a myth. There is a verse in Proverbs 16:9 that says, "We can make our plans, but the Lord determines our steps."[21]

I see that as such a profound statement about the condition of humans on this earth. It makes me want to give my attention to God instead of living in a life that is focused on self-preservation. That verse is also not a "Well, I guess it doesn't matter what I do in life because God is going to determine my steps anyway." When we realize that God knows more, cares more, and wants to help give more than we could ever plan for ourselves, we begin to trust God on another level that activates true faith and enables us to become who God has always created us to be. It is all up to us and where we decide to put that trust—in our own power and knowledge from the years we have walked this earth or in the Creator of the universe who knows us better than we know ourselves and wants to give us more than we could ever dream, imagine, ask, or think.

I am not saying that I have everything figured out with this book or even in my life , because I believe we are all changing every year we are alive. We are all on a journey, and this book represents a season of my life that I wrote out of obedience to God, and I pray it's been helpful to you. It's always important to do a self-evaluation and think about how you have changed each year of life.

---

[21] New Living Translation

Holy Crap Moment

Time for self-evaluation of some things that should matter the most in life.

Do you love more today than last year? Do you trust God more or less? Do you trust people more or less? Do you have more or less hope? Get out some paper and write down where you think you are in a few of these areas, with examples, and then keep it and look at it again in a year. See where you are in your life. God wants to help us become better in all areas of life and not just to help make us more "spiritual" (whatever that means, anyway).

Take a Moment

_____

_____

_____

_____

I would hope that I could reread my book in a few years and see how I have grown from my thinking about who I thought God was to a deeper knowledge of His grace, love, and power in my life. I pray the same for you even as you have read the words on these pages. This is not a self-help book or even a story about a guy who almost went blind and wanted to kill himself. It is my attempt to maximize what I went through to bring glory to God and shine a light on His faithfulness in my life. It is also to help people see God not as something else to add to life but the only absolute pillar of strength in times of plenty and times of need.

If you are a follower of Christ, your reaction to unexpected pain in life is the truest barometer of where you are with Jesus. I always lived life thinking that I had this radiant relationship with the God of the universe when really I was just a scared, complaining little kid when my life turned upside down. If you have read this book and are looking for comfort from a terrible situation in life, a type of crap, I only have Jesus to give you, who, in reality, is the best giver of hope we could ever ask for. If you are a follower of Christ and you are going through something difficult, then please learn from my journey and apply the principles in this book to your life. When I was going through my "little situation," I didn't want to apply *anything*. But even in that mistake I made, please learn from the things I did wrong. If you are watching someone go through crap in life, then know that no amount of worry for him or her is going to change anything. Yet your prayers and your reaching out to them and letting them know you are there can be the best medicine they could ever receive.

It has been an honor to share my story with you about the things I went through and some of the life lessons I felt God shared with me along my journey. Please stop by HolyCrapBook.com and say hello or share something encouraging with other readers of Holy Crap. Now get out of that chair you're sitting in and go love on someone. Maybe plan a trip to your local church this weekend, or just say a quiet prayer to God that you will start to trust Him in a deeper way today than you did yesterday. I know you can do it, and I am praying for you!

About the Author

BRIAN MORRIS is the General Manager of a family-friendly television station with a viewing area stretching from Denver, Colorado to Cheyenne, Wyoming. His passion in life is to see people's eternal destinies changed and their hurts healed through relevant media that challenges the status quo. He and his wife, Yolanda, have been married for over 20 years and are dedicated to changing the perception of Christian media by leading with love instead of judgment. They have lived in Colorado for over 15 years where he enjoys hiking, running, and anything technology.